Helion & Company Limited
Unit 8 Amherst Business Centre
Budbrooke Road
Warwick
CV34 5WE
England
Tel. 01926 499 619
Email: info@helion.co.uk
Website: www.helion.co.uk
Twitter: @helionbooks
https://helionbooks.wordpress.com/

Published by Helion & Company 2026

Colour figures by Adam Hook 2026
Map drawn by George Anderson © Helion & Company 2026

Cover: A group of Hwasong-9 missiles simultaneously launched on 6 March 2017. (KCBC)
Designed and typeset by Mach 3 Solutions (www.mach3solutions.co.uk)
Cover design Paul Hewitt, Battlefield Design (www.battlefield-design.co.uk)

ISBN: 978-1-806722-80-8

British Library Cataloguing-in-Publication Data
A catalogue record for this book is available from the British Library

We always welcome receiving book proposals from prospective authors.

CONTENTS

ABBREVIATIONS AND ACRONYMS

ASBM	anti-ship ballistic missile
AShM	anti-ship missile
ATGM	anti-tank guided missile
BWC	Biological Weapons Convention
CEP	circular error probable
CQC	close-quarters combat
CWC	Chemical Weapons Convention
DMZ	Korean Demilitarized Zone
DoD	Department of Defense
DPRK	Democratic People's Republic of Korea
GLCM	ground-launched cruise missile
GNSS	global navigation satellite system
GPS	Global Positioning System
HEMP	high-altitude electromagnetic pulse
HGV	hypersonic glide vehicle
IAEA	International Atomic Energy Agency
ICBM	intercontinental ballistic missile
IRBM	intermediate-range ballistic missile
IRFNA	inhibited red fuming nitric acid
KCBC	Korean Central Broadcasting Committee
KCNA	Korean Central News Agency
KPA	Korean People's Army
KPAAF	Korean People's Army Air and Anti-Air Force
KPAGF	Korean People's Army Ground Force
KPAN	Korean People's Army Navy
MANPADS	man-portable air-defence system
MaRV	manoeuvrable re-entry vehicle
MDL	Military Demarcation Line
MGB	Missile General Bureau
MIRV	multiple independently-targetable re-entry vehicle
MoD	Ministry of Defence
MRBM	medium-range ballistic missile
MRL	multiple rocket launcher
NBC	nuclear, biological, chemical
NPT	Treaty on the Non-Proliferation of Nuclear Weapons
PBV	post-boost vehicle
PRC	People's Republic of China
RGB	Reconnaissance General Bureau
ROK	Republic of Korea
ROKA	Republic of Korea Army
RPG	rocket-propelled grenade
SAM	surface-to-air missile
SLBM	submarine-launched ballistic missile
SLCM	submarine-launched cruise missile
SLV	satellite launch vehicle
SOF	Special Operations Force
SRBM	short-range ballistic missile
SSB	sub-surface ballistic (ballistic missile submarine)
SSBN	sub-surface ballistic nuclear (nuclear ballistic missile submarine)
TE	transporter erector
TEL	transporter erector launcher
THAAD	Terminal High Altitude Area Defence
UN	United Nations
US	United States
USA	United States of America
USFK	United States Forces Korea
VLS	vertical launch system
WMD	weapons of mass destruction
WPK	Workers' Party of Korea

PREFACE

The DPRK. Shrouded in mysticism and secrecy, the nation represents an absolute unicum for the military analyst. No other country in the world manages to attract so much scrutiny to its controversial antics, yet divulge so little of material importance about its inner workings. This might be at the heart of why this country specifically has gripped our attention for so many years, and drawn us to write this series about its largely mysterious armed forces.

Before we introduce the main subject, a couple of clarifications and disclaimers regarding the contents of this book. Since all claims made represent the latest analysis of current military matters in a country that is notoriously secretive, some are bound to turn out to be incorrect as new information comes to light. Wherever a claim is made that cannot be established with absolute certainty, it is clarified through appropriate qualifiers: plausible, likely, and all variations of like sort. Sources are mentioned for those claims that do not bank on our own work, when they are absent it may be assumed that the claim is either an original finding of the authors or held to be common knowledge.

As the subject we have written on mainly concerns the DPRK, it is the North Korean romanisation scheme of Korean that we have attempted to adhere to for most Korean names, which differs from those schemes common in the South. In some cases this might be cause for confusion, further clarification of what exactly is referenced is then usually provided. In similar vein, designations of the Korean People's Army's various branches are matched to their North Korean analogues, abbreviations of which are adopted as follows: Korean People's Army, KPA; Korean People's Army's Ground Force, KPAGF; Korean People's Army Air and Anti-Air Force, KPAAF; Korean People's Army Navy, KPAN; Special Operations Force, SOF; Missile General Bureau, MGB.[1] These branches also serve as the main structure of this book series, and are treated in the order listed above. We'd also like to express our profound gratitude to our dear friend Tarao, whose aid in researching and promoting this project has been indispensable. Furthermore, the variety of talented artists that have contributed to the many wonderful artworks deserve nothing but praise.[2] Any questions on this publication or related matters are more than welcome, and may be directed to onthepathofsongun@outlook.com.

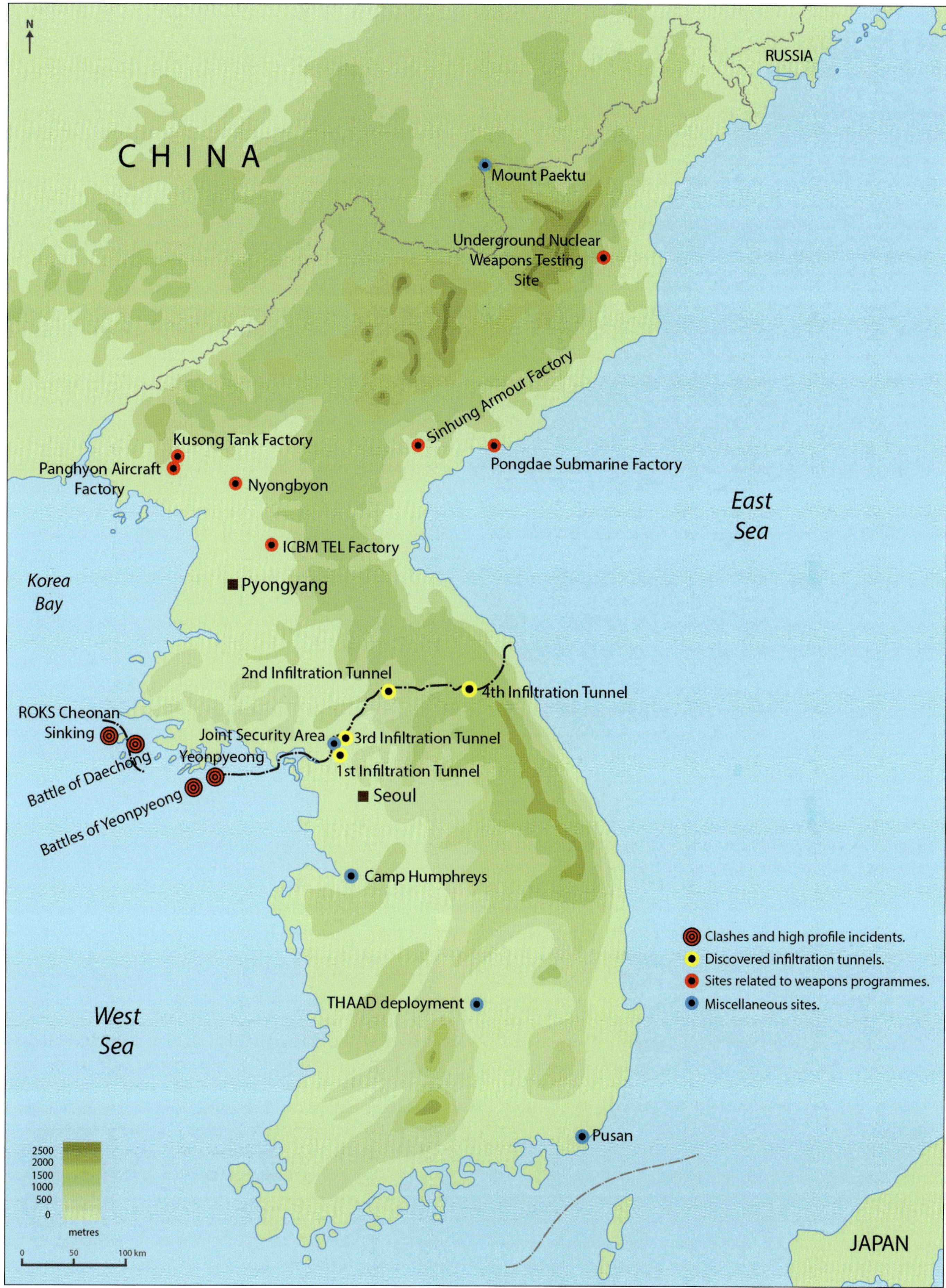

A map of North Korea with the most important locations mentioned in this volume. (Map by George Anderson)

INTRODUCTION

Tuesday, 6:02AM (GMT+9), 29 August 2017

Residents on Hokkaido, Japan's northernmost island, wake to an emergency alert on their phones. The morning dark is washed from their faces as blue-tinged screens alight. Sleepy-eyed, in bedrooms or on early commutes, they stare disbelievingly at the message as around them alarm sirens begin their unearthly wail:

> Missile launch. Missile launch. A missile has been launched from North Korea. Evacuate to a building or underground.

Though the country had over the previous decades slowly grown accustomed to the menace periodically emerging from its walled-off resting ground on the upper Korean Peninsula, 2017 had been a year unlike any other. North Korea's young leader had addressed his country in a New Year's speech and declared that preparations to launch an intercontinental ballistic missile (ICBM) had reached their final stage. In the months that followed, an unprecedented series of missile launches pushed the envelope on the North's fledgling strategic deterrent, introducing the Pukguksong-2 and Hwasong-12 to its arsenal. While both significantly escalated the threat emanating from the impoverished nation, the latter especially was alarming for its ability to strike at targets in the wider region. This includes the US territory of Guam, home of a variety of US military bases amongst which is the massive Andersen Air Force Base that routinely houses heavy strategic bombers. When on 4 July (a date that is unlikely to have been a coincidence) North Korea made good on its New Year's resolutions by testing the Hwasong-14 on a trajectory carefully avoiding surrounding countries, following up just three weeks later with a second launch, tensions began to mount. A test of the Minuteman III ICBM by the US on 2 August was construed as a tit-for-tat response (though the US conducts such tests with high regularity, the last occurring on 26 April and 2 May that year), and with the United Nations (UN) again voting to strengthen sanctions against North Korea three days later rhetoric from its state media became increasingly militant. Then US president Donald Trump seemed eager to respond in kind, and not for the first time that year B-1B bomber aircraft hailing out of Guam overflew South Korea in an apparent warning to the North. The same day, speaking from his golf club in New Jersey he made his infamous fire and fury statement:

> North Korea best not make any more threats to the United States. They will be met with fire and fury like the world has never seen. He has been very threatening beyond a normal statement. And as I said, they will be met with fire, fury and frankly power the likes of which this world has never seen before.

North Korea responded by sharply escalating its threats. In a hastily drawn up state media report it disclosed that a plan was being drawn up 'for an enveloping strike at Guam through simultaneous fire of four Hwasong-12 intermediate-range strategic ballistic rockets'. Images released on 15 August apparently depicted Kim Jong Un reviewing this strike plan, but holding off on ordering its execution to 'watch a little more the foolish and stupid conduct of the Yankees'. In the meantime, President Trump declared that 'military solutions are now fully in place, locked and loaded', and with the massive combined US-South Korean Ulchi-Freedom Guardian military exercises looming later that month East Asia seemed at the verge of its own version of its Cuban Missile Crisis.

This sequence of events preceded the missile scare of 29 August, in which North Korea (also known formally as the DPRK) launched one of its new Hwasong-12 missiles on a trajectory overflying Japan. It was the first time an explicitly military rocket was tested on such a trajectory, with the country typically choosing to avoid the repercussions such unprecedented moves can incur. Though Kim Jong Un's plans to strike the waters just off of Guam were fortunately never executed, the events of 2017 had far from reached their zenith. In the following months, North Korea consecutively conducted further missile tests, set off what it claimed to be its first thermonuclear warhead, shot another Hwasong-12 over Japan, and tested one of the largest road-mobile ICBMs ever designed: the Hwasong-15.

Provocations such as these, whether they occur close to the Korean Demilitarized Zone (DMZ) or even in entirely different nations, are the staple of inter-Korean relations and provide a stark reminder of the fact that a renewed conflict is never far away. In committing acts that fall short of outright triggering a war, the DPRK has been able to seriously influence its neighbours, and in the least retain its place in the international spotlight given that its economic and political influence are nowadays insufficient to do so. The potentially colossal humanitarian and financial catastrophe brought on by the onset of full-scale hostilities has in the past often been enough to discourage the ROK and USA from retaliating militarily, though only through exercising great restraint. Given that the economic and technological situation in the two Koreas are nowadays more in contrast than any two bordering countries in the world, the reason why this threat remains so potent might be obscure to some. However, despite the fact that in the past decades the KPA has suffered much in terms of technological prowess and overall upkeep relative to its Southern neighbour, in considering its current strength its ability to import weapons and technology from abroad (especially before the sanctions regime) is often underestimated, and the capabilities of its indigenous military industry even more so. Some of these acquisitions lean on old relations with like-minded governments, others simply exploit the black market; others still are of surprising sophistication, and suggest some larger geopolitical game is at play, presumably motivated by a Russian and Chinese desire to uphold North Korea's status as a buffer zone between these countries and Western-aligned South Korea. It is the latter category that has allowed the DPRK to reverse-engineer or otherwise copy sensitive weapons systems and technologies such as the S-300 air-defence system, Kh-35 anti-ship missile and an advanced 300mm multiple rocket launcher, not to mention a myriad of developments related to its ballistic missile programme. In more recent years, the pace at which new designs, sometimes with a clear foreign influence, at other times entirely original, have appeared is unmatched even by some major powers. Research, development and particularly the production of these systems (often within short timeframes) by the North Koreans is impressive, potentially indicative of an outside influence that has aided them. Whatever the case, it has not only enabled a revival of the KPA as a fighting force, but also helped keep the DPRK's military exports competitive during an age of ever-tightening sanctions. North Korean arms stemming from the past half-century remain abundant across the globe, and as it produces (or formerly produced) many of the weapons systems Soviet-aligned nations were supplied with, it is a source of affordable maintenance and upgrades. Its efforts at keeping these – now illegal – exports a secret constitute some of the toughest challenges to the UN in dealing with the nation, each year spawning extensive investigations and expansions of sanctions. Were it not for the unrelenting pressure exerted on other UN members to adhere to the embargoes in place, North Korea would likely be a major arms exporter, generating much revenue for a state known for its economic hardship, as well as allowing it to regain some of the influence decades of isolation have bereft it of. Of course, the days where the DPRK could boast of substantial economic gains and widespread political clout have long gone. In an age then where its adversaries enjoy a massive technological and economical advantage, and its traditional allies for the first time show hesitation in their resolve, the two branches of the KPA specialising in unconventional warfare seem ever more central to its continued relevance. As the North's special forces continue to evade the spotlight however, the question remains: Will they wither in the shadow of North Korea's blooming nuclear arsenal, or will stubborn adherence to the Songun (military first) doctrine allow them to soldier on?

CHAPTER 1

SPECIAL OPERATIONS FORCE

North Korea's special operations forces are often touted as being the largest in the world, with a force of 200,000 ready to strike at South Korea, Japan and beyond as soon as they are given the order. However, for all the mythical proportions it is often credited with, a lack of accurate information on North Korea's special operations forces as well as its intelligence apparatus has led to a skewed image of their numbers and what the true numbers actually represent. Nevertheless, both are set to play a major role during any conflict the DPRK might find itself in, and the threat they pose is considerable both during wartime and peacetime. For all the secrecy surrounding their numbers and operations, North Korea's special operations forces and intelligence agencies are also responsible for one of the three pillars for conquering the South: they are tasked with creating a Second Front in the Republic of Korea's (ROK) strategic rear, and supporting the advance of the 'One Blow Non-Stop Attack' as North Korean forces move deeper into the South. To secure their entry into South Korea and Japan, the special operations forces utilise a wide range of specialised aircraft, ships, submarines and also more unconventional means to reach their objective safely and undetected. After having arrived at their objectives, they are to be employed for strategic, operational and tactical level operations, which would see the destruction of key military and civilian targets as well as infrastructure to hinder the Republic of Korea Army's (ROKA) advance towards the DMZ, the assassination of military and political figures and identification of targets for artillery and ballistic missiles. Furthermore, they would be employed to support regular army operations, and also to draw away attention and keep ROKA forces occupied that could otherwise be used at the frontline.

In line with these important objectives, the North has invested heavily in expanding the numbers, capabilities and training of its special operations forces to meet the challenges of twenty-first century warfare. This has mainly manifested itself through a large influx of more modern weaponry compared to regular Korean People's Army's Ground Force (KPAGF) forces, but also increasing night time, urban and mountaineering training, the latter two of which are especially important with the geography of South Korea in mind.[1] The special operations forces are also unique due to the fact that it is the only branch that can be expanded and modernised without significant costs or running into significant technological difficulties such as a modernisation of the Korean People's Army Air and Anti-Air Force (KPAAF) or Missile General Bureau (MGB) requires. Since its virtues lie mainly in asymmetric warfare, which the DPRK utilises to full advantage in all of its military branches, it is thus highly likely that investments in the special operations forces will continue to mount. Accompanying these investments have been several reorganisations with the aim of improving the organisational structure of its special forces, marked by the XI 'Storm' Corps, formerly known as Light Infantry Training Guidance Bureau, and the VIII Special Purpose Corps, becoming an independent branch akin to the air force and strategic force under the name of Special Operations Force.[2] However, most other KPA branches and the intelligence agencies themselves maintain their own, separate special operations forces units as well – a structure resulting from the plurality of branches of the KPA and the wide-ranging missions the special operations forces are to be involved in. This reveals itself primarily in a clear distinction between the various forces, most notably the strategic SOF and light infantry units. Accounting for their strategic role, the primary task of the former is to be inserted into the South and Japan by aircraft and ships in order to establish a Second Front and carry out their objectives in the strategic rear. The primary objective of the light infantry units is navigating difficult terrain prior to the arrival of mechanised forces or in areas where mechanised operations are all but impossible, for seizing and defending key infrastructure such as bridges and tunnels, allowing them to maintain their quick advance into the South; a highly important task if a North Korean invasion is to succeed in its initial

Kim Jong Un inspects SOF soldiers prior to a maritime exercise. (KCBC)

plans. These are literally light infantry, lighter equipped and faster on foot than regular troops but still fighting in the conventional infantry role. While the strategic SOF and light infantry units have certain overlapping tasks, the latter should be seen as distinct from special operations forces and is more accurately represented through its own count rather than to be thrown in with SOF numbers. This means that the oft-mentioned number of SOF personnel of some 180,000 to 200,000 is in actuality just some 60,000, with the roughly 120,000 remaining personnel belonging to the light infantry units.

Light Infantry

Although truthfully the light infantry are in a very different class than the SOF, that North Korea attaches great value to these units has been made clear by the establishment of new light infantry units for the KPAGF's Forward Corps, and enlarging current ones. Most notably, existing light infantry brigades were expanded to regiment size and seven regular infantry divisions were reorganised to light infantry divisions during the early 2000s.[3] What has resulted is a force that in numbers alone surpasses the size of many entire militaries in the world, albeit one that is in fact locked behind a heavily fortified border complete with anti-personnel mines: the Military Demarcation Line (MDL). While the past has shown that the DMZ which surrounds it can be stealthily navigated by small groups of infiltrators, it prevents the movement of large troop numbers between either Korea. It is thus perhaps not surprising that the North not only intends to sneak across the DMZ by ground, go over it by air and circumvent it by sea, but also to go under it through tunnels.

These tunnels, nicknamed the 'Tunnels of Aggression' by South Korea, would be the primary route of the light infantry units into the South during wartime. While their relevance in the current military environment is sometimes judged to be low due to proper intelligence and the targeting of their entrances, their existence is directly linked to the light infantry units' capability to cross into the Southern portion of the DMZ safely and undetected and thereby remain a highly potent and important asset for the North. To further emphasise the importance that North Korea attaches to these tunnels, Kim Il Sung is reported to have said that 'one tunnel would be more effective than ten atomic bombs' before giving the order to commence tunnelling under the DMZ in 1971, which supposedly began the following year.[4] [5] The efforts that have gone into building these tunnels must have been extensive, and experience gained with the construction of the secretive Pyongyang metro, which was finished at around the same time that tunnelling into the South started, is sure to have been of use. Sloping upwards towards the South in order to allow water to drain back to North Korea, their entrances in the DPRK are believed to extend up to 100 metres vertically into the ground and are well hidden. On the other end, their entrance would likely not be drilled to the surface until hostilities commenced, so as to maintain their secrecy.

The discovery of the first tunnel occurred in November 1974 after a ROKA army patrol noticed steam rising out of the ground in the western sector of the DMZ near Gorangpo, 65 kilometres north of Seoul.[6] After finding a hatch, and being fired upon from across the DMZ, they soon uncovered a concrete-reinforced tunnel complete with a narrow-gauge railway that ran 0.45 metres below ground for an estimated length of 3.5 kilometres, extending one kilometre south of the MDL. At 1.2 metres wide and 0.9 metres high, the tunnel was equipped with storage and sleeping areas and could be used to transport an entire regiment each hour. North Korean efforts at concealing their labours were extensive, and a booby trap tragically claimed two lives (one South Korean and one American), wounding several others in the process. While this tunnel was initially seen as simply an elaborate contraption to facilitate the secret entry of North Korean infiltrators into the South, two North Korean defectors claimed in 1975 that they had been working on several tunnels running under the MDL.[7] Furthermore, they revealed that these were in fact not mere infiltration tunnels, but rather full-blown invasion tunnels with the supposed capacity to quickly insert tens of thousands of troops into the South. One of the defectors stated that he had personally seen the construction of nine tunnels, and that there were probably two such large tunnels dug for each of the 10 North Korean infantry divisions then deployed near the border. Now looking out for up to 20 invasion tunnels, the ROK quickly commenced a search alongside the DMZ to investigate the veracity of the defectors' claims.

The first known tunnel would soon be joined by others, for a total of four confirmed. The next discovery came fairly quickly after the first, after South Korean troops reported hearing explosions directly beneath the ground of their positions. Several exploration

A photo taken inside the first infiltration tunnel discovered in 1974. The narrow-gauge railway was originally built to transport concrete blocks through the tunnel as its construction progressed, but could also be used to move soldiers and their equipment if the need arose. (Korean Overseas Information Service)

The 1974 infiltration tunnel ran less than a half a metre below ground. (KTV)

boreholes drilled into the ground confirmed the soldiers' suspicions, and an interception tunnel broke through at a depth of 50 metres underground in March 1975.[8] Almost twice as wide and high as the previous one discovered, this tunnel was dug through granite at a depth of 50 to 160 metres, negating the need for concrete reinforcements. Also of an estimated 3.5 kilometres length and located some 100 kilometres away from Seoul, this tunnel was said to allow the passage of a full division, or roughly 30,000 troops, in just one hour. Although this number is likely to be inflated, the fact that an entire troop assembly area was also carved out in the tunnel does affirm the difference in scale and utility. The North Koreans, after finding out that the South had discovered the second tunnel, hastily began to place booby-trapped obstacles along the length of it as the South Koreans progressed their search. After this failed to halt them, they then sealed off part of the tunnel with reinforced concrete. The location of a third tunnel was suspected after a large underground explosion in June 1978 as well as reports from a defector, but its exact location was only found four months later in October 1978. Forty-four kilometres from Seoul and some four kilometres South of Panmunjom (the 'Peace Village', and also the location of the Joint Security Area (JSA)), it was similar in size and construction to tunnel two.[9] Nevertheless, it was just 1.6 kilometres long, running 435 metres south of the MDL at a depth of 73 metres. Supposedly, coal dust was smeared on its walls in order to disguise the tunnel as an abandoned coal mine, though of course these efforts would have been quite unconvincing. In direct contrast with the swift succession of discoveries during the 1970s, the 1980s revealed no further tunnels underneath the DMZ. Whether this was the result of improved, more silent construction techniques, improved operations security or mere chance is unknown, but South Korean ground measurements after the initial discoveries indicating that over 20 additional tunnels may exist did spur searches with more advanced equipment. Even with these extended efforts, it would take until March 1990 for the fourth and last tunnel to be found near Yanggu, much closer to the eastern coast than the previous ones. Believed to be roughly two kilometres long, it was largely identical to tunnels two and three, meaning they were likely to have all been constructed at the same time and to a similar design template. Although the previous discoveries prompted denials from the North Koreans, who claimed they were either South Korean fabrications, or abandoned Japanese coal mines, despite the presence of North Korean paraphernalia in all tunnels and North Korean slogans found inscribed on the walls, a surprisingly frank admission of the purpose of the fourth tunnel followed in 1990. Broadcasted across the DMZ, it was supposedly claimed that the tunnel was constructed to 'facilitate peaceful reunification' by 'replacing the concrete wall' the South was alleged to have built.[10] The discovery of the fourth tunnel also confirmed the North had dug tunnels along the entire length of the DMZ, once again lending credence to the theory that each of the (at the time) 10 infantry divisions along the border could utilise two major tunnels during wartime.

Despite reports of as many as dozens of additional tunnels, none were publicly discovered following the events of 1990. Whether this was the result of the location and construction techniques used in the remaining tunnels, the desire to keep additional discoveries a secret or simply the fact that no other tunnels exist is unknown. However, evidence of more tunnels continues to discredit the latter possibility, and the United States Forces Korea (USFK) Eighth US Army G-2 Tunnel Neutralization Team identified between 25 and 30 suspected new tunnels by 1987, mainly concentrated near Cholwon – one of the main avenues of approach during an invasion of the South.[11] Two dozen still undetected tunnels could collectively allow hundreds of thousands of troops to cross large swathes of the DMZ undetected, giving the KPA the drop on the South in the initial stages of a conflict. It has been speculated that the last three tunnels captured could also be used to insert small vehicles and artillery beyond the MDL, but

The second infiltration tunnel featured several carved out sections throughout its length to allow units to regroup or pass one another. (Korean Overseas Information Service)

Two ROKA soldiers stand guard to counter any North Korean response to the discovery of the fourth infiltration tunnel. (Korean Overseas Information Service)

although they were large enough to accommodate small vehicles and artillery in theory, it is questionable if the entrances or exits would facilitate their use, let alone if this was ever envisaged by the North. It is possible that other tunnels allowing for the movement of vehicles, including armoured fighting vehicles and artillery exist, as the minefields and anti-tank ditches in and around the DMZ would be very difficult to cross. These would likely require ventilation, more sturdy construction and therefore far more investment at a higher risk however, and it is doubtful if the advantages would be deemed to outweigh that.

Nonetheless, the search for new tunnels continues to this day both by the military and civilian enthusiasts, to no apparent success. In South Korea this has led to somewhat of a cult around the subject, with some devoting their entire life to searching for tunnels not only along the border but even in the heart of Seoul, claiming for instance that they are connected to sewers in the capital. The discovered tunnels themselves are nowadays popular tourist destinations near the DMZ, with tours available of all but the first tunnel. Since constructing them in the 1970s and 1980s must have cost the North considerable expenses, the irony that they have now become sources of income to the South is palpable.

It is possible that as yet undiscovered tunnels could also be used for the insertion of infiltrators during peacetime. While this would be substantially easier than navigating the entirety of the DMZ, the DPRK might be hard pressed to risk the uncovering of a tunnel for the insertion of a single infiltrator especially as other alternatives are available. Still, a prelude to war might see the tunnels used in this manner, with infiltrators for instance dressed in ROKA uniforms being able to sow confusion amongst the ranks while the actual invasion is set up. For deeper insertion missions the tunnels are not of much use: their relatively short length, which does not even span the entire DMZ in the cases that have been uncovered, means they are ill-suited for the creation of the so-called Second Front, which would be located in the strategic rear of the ROK. However, the tunnels might retain their use even as fighting progresses. Although they are not built as such, they could be easily transformed into difficult to spot and highly durable fortifications later on in a war. The DPRK is not unfamiliar with such tunnel warfare, and notably used it with success during the Battle of Heartbreak Ridge in the Korean War, which is still touted as a major victory in North Korean propaganda.[12] Nevertheless, the main use of the tunnels underneath the DMZ remains to facilitate the movement of light infantry units, for which purpose they remain a difficult to assess but potentially highly effective means. Should a war suddenly break out, the continued presence of 20 or more of these tunnels, many of which may be capable of facilitating the movement of thousands to tens of thousands of troops per hour, could have tremendous effects on the battlefield. On the other hand, if they have readily been identified and countermeasures have been prepared, they could well become death traps for their users instead.

Tunnels are far from the only means available to the light infantry units for carrying out their mission across the DMZ however, and at least some are also trained for airborne and airmobile insertion, and would be responsible for carrying out some of the more SOF-like objectives these units are tasked with.[13] Wartime scenarios would see these airborne light infantry units dropped further behind enemy lines to secure or destroy infrastructure, conduct reconnaissance and eliminate threats to the main force, such as artillery, out of reach of the light infantry units that advance through or under the DMZ on foot. However, their mission area remains closer to the main force than that of the strategic SOF. Given their importance in securing the advance of the KPA, each Forward Corps has two light infantry brigades that would operate ahead of the main force in designated sectors. The common factor between all light infantry units is that they are lightly equipped and lack any kind of supporting firepower, which prevents them from directly facing well-equipped ROKA units one-on-one. Their primary tasks require them to avoid direct confrontations with the ROKA, leaving their destruction to regular KPA units. However, they could overwhelm defensive positions by exploiting their massive numbers early on in an invasion should the need arise. Portable weaponry such as anti-tank guided missiles (ATGMs), man-portable air-defence systems (MANPADS), and mortars, as well as sporadic artillery support, gives them some ability to directly take on lighter-equipped ROKA units especially in poorly navigable terrain. After their preparatory work along the DMZ is completed and initial mobilisation has enabled regular KPA units to commence the invasion proper, the main thrust would make full use of the work done by the light infantry units and make haste towards the Southern capital. This pattern would repeat in other difficult to navigate areas encountered during the southward push, whereby light infantry would move in advance of regular KPA units and pave the way for the bulk of the armed forces. Near the eastern seaboard, where the terrain is generally more wooded and mountainous, the light infantry units would also bear responsibility for the bulk of the fighting in areas that preclude the effective deployment of heavy weaponry.

Special Operations Forces

The not entirely dissimilar, yet ultimately quite separate, special operations forces of the DPRK are organised around the Special Operations Force, which comprises three sniper brigades, four light infantry brigades and three airborne light infantry brigades (often referred to as 'Bolt', 'Lightning' and 'Thunder, respectively). Although they differ from each other in specific tasks and tactics, the brigades of the special operations forces are mainly geared towards special operations and operations in the strategic rear of the South, differentiating them from their namesakes subordinate to the KPAGF. Not all SOF are directly subordinate to the SOF branch however, and the KPAAF and KPAN operate two sniper brigades each (airborne and amphibious, respectively), while the KPA's General Staff Department and KPAGF also have a number of dedicated SOF units subordinate to their command.[14] Some sources additionally list three sniper brigades under the Reconnaissance General Bureau (RGB), but their jurisdiction with regards to such SOF units cannot be verified, although they do operate a number of SOF reconnaissance battalions. Altogether, close to 100 SOF battalions exist with a total strength of 60,000 personnel. Despite not coming even near the oft-reported figure of 200,000, this is still a very impressive number, unparalleled by any equivalents abroad.

The Special Operations Force contributes the largest portion to the total SOF strength, and by the virtue of its numbers and training it is the most important special forces asset of the North. They are trained to operate in all environments (land, air and sea) and their motivation ranks among the highest of the KPA. The principal focus of this force lies in the strategic rear of the ROK, and possibly even Japan, aiming to engage in operations on all three levels of scale:

Strategic level: operations of which include disabling or securing Command, Control, Communication, Computers and Intelligence (C4I) assets, which specifically entails the assassination of ROK government and military officials.

Operational level: operations that see to the destruction of major military targets such as airfields, ports, supply depots and other bases.

Tactical level: operations in support of regular army advances, and which for instance aim to encircle enemy columns, assault fortifications and conduct reconnaissance missions.

These serve not only to disorient decision-making in the South, disable military assets available and thwart defensive operations, it also ties up ROKA forces in the strategic rear, preventing their effective use on the frontlines.

Assassination missions are especially important to the SOF, and no other military in the world is believed to have integrated assassination missions into their doctrine to the extent that the DPRK has. During wartime this means not only high-ranking government and military officials are to be targeted for assassination and kidnapping, but also mayors or others in government positions that are not necessarily directly linked to the war effort. Supposedly, this means in practice that each company of the Special Operations Force is assigned a major city in the ROK to conduct operations in, with an assassination brigade tasked with killing or kidnapping the mayor and other officials, whereas others in patrolling brigades would seek to take control of local media infrastructure, execute bombings and conduct reconnaissance.[15] Multiple levels of redundancy would be introduced to ensure success, with most important officials having three separate squads dedicated to their assassination. These assassinations would also be politically motivated to some degree: leaving unharmed only those politicians that favour rapprochement with the North to ensure a favourable political climate in which a pro-North Korean government could be set up with some legitimacy to Southerners. SOF operations are likely to overlap with those of the intelligence agencies, which have significant experience with kidnapping and assassination operations during peacetime.

Of course, perhaps the most-high profile of these assassinations would target the South Korean president in the opening stages of a war. Although this could well be a mission delegated to the RGB, SOF units were extensively covered in an exercise which simulated a strike on the ROK's Blue House, during which a downscaled replica of the president's office and residence was obliterated. Although the December 2016 exercise was clearly not geared towards realism – featuring several symbolic acts of destruction as well as implausible tactics such as insertion by parachute and helicopters yet extraction by car and motorcycle, while multiple rocket launchers (MRLs) bombarded the Blue House – the threat conveyed is certainly real. In fact, one of the most famous acts of peacetime terrorism entailed raiding the Blue House in an actual attempt on then president Park Chung Hee's life. Conducted on 21 January 1968, during the height of tensions between the two nations, 31 North Korean commandos infiltrated the ROK and made their way to within sight of the Blue House before the plan went awry. After a manhunt of several days all but two of the infiltrators had been killed or committed suicide, with one captured and another escaping back into the North.[16] On the opposing side, 26 South Koreans and four Americans were killed, with many more left wounded including dozens of civilians. Response to the raid was limited due to the USS *Pueblo* incident which occurred just two days later, but it did spawn the creation of the ROKA's infamous Unit 684 which was tasked with the assassination of Kim Il Sung, yet ultimately mutinied leaving dozens dead. On the North Korean side, the raid provided some interesting information about the modus operandi of North Korean SOF and the threat they posed. Training of the elite North Korean Unit 124 was intense and prolonged, and favourable political inclination appears to have been imperative in its composition. After a two-year training period, which also saw the use of a full-scale mock-up of the Blue House, they crossed the DMZ on 17 January, entering Seoul on 20 January. Equipped with a variety of weaponry including Soviet PPS-43 submachine guns, handguns and anti-tank and fragmentation grenades, the team then utilised accurate ROKA uniforms to aid their infiltration. Four civilians identified them nevertheless on the 19th and notified the authorities.[17] This strategy is highly notable, as it is believed North Korean infiltrators would make use of ROKA uniforms and concealed weapons extensively during wartime operations in an attempt to disrupt operations, thus requiring intricate security protocols as a responsive measure.

Such use has been noted on many occasions during infiltration attempts of the past, and the previous South Korean service rifle, the M16A1, was found to be carried by multiple infiltrators during the 1990s. Although some of these appeared to be US-manufactured examples (presumably acquired from Vietnam), others were specifically produced or retooled to imitate the minor deviations the South Korean-manufactured examples had from regular M16A1s. Nowadays, new uniforms and the plethora of more modern weaponry now used by regular ROKA units complicates such deception efforts, and different strategies such as simply using civilian clothes may be used instead in time of war. Concealed weaponry has often been used in conjunction with this option, typically in the form of the

Among the primary objectives of North Korea's SOF is the elimination of high-value targets located in South Korea and possibly even Japan. Thwarting the activities of such assassination squads before they execute their plans will require abundant manpower and resources. (KCBC)

It may be presumed that North Korean SOF and infiltrators will attempt to make use of vehicles mimicking those used by the ROK to sow further confusion among enemy ranks, like these North Korean soldiers clad in ROKA uniforms atop a US-pattern military jeep. (KCBC)

Czechoslovakian vz. 61 machine pistol or handguns like the FN Baby Browning, usually equipped with suppressors (and invariably so in the latter case). The M16A1 was largely phased out of service in the ROKA in favour of the South Korean K2 rifle, and is now only used by reserve forces, and will hence likely have fallen out of use in the North as well. However, there are still some indications that North Korea attempts to infiltrate its Southern neighbour using accurate ROKA uniforms and weaponry. In one specific incident, a South Korean soldier is said to have seen North Korean soldiers dressed in South Korean 'Granite' pixelated camouflage uniforms and armed with K2 rifles moving into positions along the DMZ during the sporadic artillery clashes in 2015.[18] Although it should have been possible for North Korea to set up its own production lines for ROKA uniforms, another possible source of these is neighbouring China, where illegal copies of various military uniforms (including the ROKA's 'Granite' pixelated pattern) are known to be produced. Smuggling from the West is another effective option, as attested by a California-based Chinese national tasked with obtaining military uniforms for DPRK subterfuge operations in the 2020s.[19] In the early 2020s, a copy of the 'Granite-B' pattern was seen in use with regular units on parade in Pyongyang, showing that it is now also being introduced beyond infiltrator units. While it is generally believed that the North is in the possession of (copied) K2 rifles, how it first acquired one is still a matter of debate. In one incident in 1997, a 'Major Baek' entered the barracks of the ROKA's 51st Infantry Division and requested one of the soldiers' K2 rifles and two magazines for a patrol before leaving.[20] [21] Despite an active search for 'Major Baek' and his real identity, neither the Major nor the K2 rifle were ever found, leading some to think that this was in fact a North Korean intelligence operative on a mission to acquire a K2 rifle for North Korea to reverse engineer. Whether this theory is true or not, the DPRK could easily have acquired examples from one of the many nations currently using the rifle across the globe.

Other missions on the operational level include attacking key targets, preferably those lightly defended or vulnerable to infiltrations, such as airports. While most air bases in the ROK are well-defended by ground forces, in concert with artillery and missile strikes, and infiltration in ROKA uniform, such missions could well succeed. Alternatively, forces could move to the vicinity of airports and use MANPADS to target aircraft, possibly using caches already present in the ROK. Light mortars could also be used to deal extensive damage to air bases as well as fuel and ammunition depots, which are especially vulnerable to such attacks. Artillery and ballistic missile units are also a likely target, although their mobility means they present a tougher target for SOF units which travel afoot. Both civilian and military infrastructure such as airports, railroads and bridges will be targeted in order to prevent the ROK and US from transporting supplies and reinforcements to the frontline, substantially hindering their ability to respond to North Korean offensives when properly executed. More difficult objectives, such as command centres, are also certain to be on the target list, and successful infiltration or destruction would have a potentially severely disruptive effect.

On the tactical level, the main task of SOF units is in carrying out reconnaissance missions of enemy positions, troop movements and high-value targets. In this task it is aided by at least seven deep artillery reconnaissance battalions and seven reconnaissance battalions under the RGB, the jurisdiction of which overlaps with SOF units on this point.[22] These missions are of vital importance for target acquisition for air, artillery, and ballistic missile strikes, which are dependent on known coordinates for their efficacy. Although other methods, including the use of reconnaissance drones, are used for these purposes in other countries, these have begun to proliferate more widely only in the 2020s, such that ground reconnaissance remains the predominant tactic.

Contrary to many other special forces around the world, and in reflection of the policies in other branches of the KPA, the SOF also recruits women, who are to conduct combat operations alongside their male counterparts. Training is harsh and given the range of possible situations they could face in the ROK, very extensive, including further specialised training for units with special tasks. Special forces frequently feature in training exercises aired by North Korean state TV under the guise of 'Large Combined Unit 630'. However, the footage is perhaps more famous for them walking and rolling on glass splinters, destroying bricks with their bare hands, endlessly punching wooden beams and trees, hitting each other with swords and axes and jumping through burning loops. Although this training has been subject of much mockery and its effectiveness on combat performance is questionable, it does aid in the creation of a well-motivated, fearless and disciplined soldier. More practical firearms and vehicle training also occurs, as well as comprehensive exercises in the North Korean martial art of Kyoksul. As many as 14 urban warfare training centres are available for CQC exercises, with the mid-2020s bringing a notable uptick in training for realistic combat scenarios, including through the use of combat simulation gear similar to the Multiple Integrated Laser Engagement System (MILES).[23]

Kim Il Sung is informed on the differences between the Type-68 and Type-88 assault rifles employed by the KPA and the M16A1 rifle and M2 carbine used by the ROKA somewhere during the 1980s. (KCBC)

A North Korean soldier deployed as part of the country's COVID-19 response efforts is clad in the North's version of the South Korean Granite-B camouflage pattern. It is anticipated that North Korean SOF will heavily utilise this replicated pattern during times of conflict. (KCBC)

North Korean SOF units at an urban warfare training centre in March 2025. Equipment includes body armour, a FAST-type helmet with tactical flashlight and headset, and a Type-88 with blank fire adaptor and 'jungle-style' (taped) magazines. Note the GoPro fixed to the iron sights in the middle, possibly for subsequent evaluation. (KCBC)

The general level of fitness, ideological motivation, and qualities as logistically independent light infantry made North Korean SOF units the candidate of choice for deployment in support of Russia's invasion of Ukraine starting in late 2024. While reports of North Korean technical personnel and advisors (especially related to the deployment of Hwasong-11B ballistic missiles) had circulated for much of the preceding year, verifiable evidence only began emerging in October of 2024. From that month onwards, as per South Korean and US estimates as many as 11,000 (or four brigades) SOF personnel were first transferred to the Russian Far East for training and outfitting and next shipped to the Kursk region. Here they were reportedly embedded with the 106th Guards Airborne Division, 155th Naval Infantry Brigade, 11th Air Assault Brigade, and the 810th Guards Naval Infantry Division, rather than constituting their own separate units.[24] While initial assessments suggested the units were composed entirely of XI 'Storm' Corps brigades, the presence of RGB units was later confirmed as well. Exclusively utilising modern Russian and civilian-market equipment, they first participated in large-scale offensives in January, suffering heavy casualties especially to drone warfare in exchange for meagre territorial gains. While identification was complicated by the carrying of false IDs and documents, the recovery of various North Korean dialect notebooks and materials as well as the capture of two personnel left little doubt about their true origin.[25] Reporting on the SOF's performance was mixed, with some noting that they lacked Russian language skills, applicable training and familiarisation with drones. However, the soldiers were generally described by soldiers on both sides of the conflict as well-motivated, fit, and relentless in their ideological conviction to the point of rarely allowing themselves to be captured alive. In fact, no more than two North Koreans were captured during 2024 and 2025, reportedly due to a lack of means to commit suicide. Moreover, they were ascribed excellent marksmanship and the ability to adapt quickly. While the large infantry-only assaults across open fields have at times diminutively been described as 'human wave tactics', such independent operations are in fact in line with the SOF's role in the DPRK. The flat open spaces and thoroughly surveilled battle grounds around Sudzha are a poor match for North Korean training however, and with the comparatively small numbers involved there was little chance of the North Korean contingent forcing a breakthrough. While total casualty numbers are difficult to estimate, they have been undeniably severe, with South Korean intelligence claiming 2,700 wounded and 300 killed after mere weeks of fighting.[26] In response, at least 3,000 additional personnel including mechanised infantry, engineering and electronic reconnaissance units were reportedly newly deployed between January and February.[27] During 2025, these units were primarily deployed to (recaptured) Kursk, engaging in construction, mine clearing and C-UAS training. According to Russian sources, they numbered some 5,000 construction workers and 1,000 deminers by mid-2025, returning to North Korea in December that year.[28] Claims of new deployments in late 2025 on the frontlines in Ukraine cannot be verified, nor did reports that an additional 25,000 to 30,000 troops would be sent materialise that year. Meanwhile, the SOF's light infantry brigades are likely to have returned home in a diminished capacity, leaving North Korea with substantial gaps in its most elite forces. Those that returned will bring valuable new knowledge (especially in counter-drone tactics) as well as the rare commodity of actual combat experience however, which if properly exploited can ultimately enhance effectiveness to a substantial degree by informing future training and innovations. Also of interest is the fact that returning units were apparently allowed to retain their Russian equipment, resulting in a not-insignificant influx of Russian-made uniforms, body armour, and Russian-manufactured AK-12 assault rifles with 1P87 collimator sights. Other equipment used by North Korean soldiers in Kursk, but not yet spotted in the DPRK, include the Chukavin sniper rifle, Vepr-12 semi-automatic shotgun, RPK-74, RMG multipurpose rocket weapon, and a captured Mk 19 automatic grenade launcher.

Equipment tends to be the best available to the entire KPA, which is evident not only in the quality but also quantity of specialised clothing such as knee-pads, helmets, body armour and tactical vests, which are generally lacking for regular units. In recent years, small arms have consisted mainly of the Type-88 and their shortened/bullpup variants, with some modified for use with the new helical magazines or as part of the 'NK11' multi-weapon, both of which are entering service in increasing numbers. Going forward, SOF units might also become the first recipients of AK-12/19 copies when they enter service. For diver squads, a unique grappling hook munition (seemingly compatible with the standard rifle grenade barrel end piece) was developed

Members of a North Korean sapper unit operating an MT-10 Stalker demining robot raise their guns in response to a simulated FPV drone threat during deployment in the Kursk region. (All-Russian Public Organization "Russia")

A squad of North Korean paratroopers aim a small-calibre mortar at a target during an exercise. Lightweight and small in size, these mortars give the paratroopers a limited stand-off capability against enemy forces and targets such as fuel dumps or munition depots. (KCBC)

North Korean soldiers belonging to an 'Overseas Operations Unit' (believed to be XI Corps or RGB personnel) march with Russian-made AK-12 assault rifles during the 2025 parade celebrating the 80th anniversary of the founding of the WPK. (KCBC)

Soldiers practice pushing an iron bar between their necks, a popular 'exercise' often performed in front of the North Korean leadership and other important figures. (KCBC)

Kim Jong Un poses with a special forces trainee wielding a suppressed Steyr SSG 08 copy (possibly chambered in 7.62x54mmR) with original Schmidt & Bender optic, at a special operation training base in August 2025. (KCBC)

that can be fired with a blank cartridge to facilitate boarding of naval vessels. More specialised firearms designed for combat divers include various underwater guns, possibly also including a copy of the APS underwater assault rifle, one of which was found on a North Korean agent attempting to smuggle it out of Russia in 1995.[29] For close-quarters combat (CQC) fighting they are alongside some AFV operators among the few KPA personnel to be issued submachine guns, consisting of older Škorpion vz. 61-based examples or a more modern design resembling the Russian PP-19 Vityaz. Heavier weaponry consists of rocket-propelled grenades (RPGs) and grenade launchers as well as lightweight (60mm) mortars, alongside the Type-73 general-purpose machine gun and Type-78 designated marksman rifle. Modern sniper rifles are also entering service, with rifles like a precise copy of the Steyr SSG 08 unveiled in April 2025 explicitly declared to be intended for SOF units. These rifles are currently used by sniper units under the 91 Capital Defence Corps as well as the Ministry of State Security. Furthermore, they are seemingly a key part of efforts to increase the prevalence of sniper units in the whole army, with a dedicated Central Sniper Training Center under the KPA's General Staff in the works to replace this function at special operation training bases.[30]

Statements made by Kim Jong Un during a test of loitering munitions in 2024 suggest that small man-portable loitering munitions are under development for SOF use. Obviously, a variety of grenades (including the US M26 grenade) and explosives, as well as a pistol (which regular soldiers are not typically issued) are also carried together with typical equipment. The SOF is also the only branch to use night-vision devices in significant numbers. Although there have been numerous reports of North Korea attempting to import such devices (including from Cuba and the USA), the variant that appears to have been most widely deployed seems to be at least partly of indigenous manufacture.[31] The use of heavier equipment than listed above is constrained by the fact that a large portion of SOF would be inserted by parachute and would have to traverse large distances afoot, and although they are trained to do so with heavy gear this all but precludes the carrying of heavy mortars, MANPADS or ATGMs. Additionally, for troops operating in the strategic rear, ease of concealment would be a factor, as well as the fact that resupplies are unlikely to occur. These would therefore either be equipped with weaponry capable of using munitions found in the South, or simply be forced to pick up armament wherever possible.

A combat swimmer fires a grappling hook munition at a simulated enemy naval vessel before boarding. While the wartime efficiency of this tactic seems limited, it could potentially be effective during the infiltration of enemy harbours. (KCBC)

SOF soldiers hold their bullpup variants of the Type-88 assault rifle as they wade through a shallow patch of water. (KCBC)

A North Korean sniper duo operating a suppressed Type-78 during exercises in 2025. The use of the Type-78 almost certainly mirrored designated marksman practices seen in aligned nations at first, but has begun to shift towards Western standards in recent years. Note that the original Type-78 was probably not compatible with suppressors, thus implying several modifications were made. (KCBC)

SOF are restricted to using armaments they can carry with them, such as the Bulsae-2 ATGM launcher shown on the back of a soldier of the Izz ad-Din al-Qassam Brigades, the military wing of Hamas in Gaza. A dedicated carrying system for two missiles is also known to be employed by North Korea. (Izz ad-Din al-Qassam Brigades)

Further specialised equipment for command, control, communications, computers, intelligence, surveillance and reconnaissance (C4ISR) and more niche applications is also believed to be in greater use with SOF than regular units. This includes modern radio equipment, but also personal (touchscreen) data devices for networking and even portable radars for target acquisition. The diversity of such equipment in use underlines the wide-ranging tasks of the SOF as well as their importance to KPA doctrine. One particularly interesting example of this is North Korea's adaptation of a weapon banned by the Convention on Certain Conventional Weapons (to which it is not a signatory): the laser rifle. An incident in 2003 where two US Army Apache helicopters flying along the southern side of the DMZ were illuminated by such a weapon had already indicated that the North Koreans were adopting this concept, though the particulars of the system in question long remained uncertain.[32] Its inclusion in an arms brochure would later unveil a relatively bulky weapon with a Bushnell Yardage Pro riflescope, weighing 14.4 kilogrammes in total, effective out to 600 metres and reportedly 'for making the enemy's eyesight lose who are aiming or monitoring our forces'.[33]

One of North Korea's laser rifle designs, which is offered for export and likely also utilised to a limited extent within the country itself. (Wingman Media)

Insertion of SOF in wartime would occur through airdrops from aircraft and helicopters or amphibious operations from simple speedboats, hovercraft/landing craft or more specialised infiltration craft. Nonetheless, despite the copious amounts of resources dedicated to this purpose, numbering some 300 An-2s, 150 Mi-2s and Mi-4s and up to 200 large hovercraft, the transport capabilities remain insufficient to meet the demands of North Korea's massive SOF. This highlights the most important challenge to both this key branch of the KPA and its Sniper Brigades: ensuring the arrival of its forces in their primary area of operations in the ROK's strategic rear. Although up to some 13,000 personnel could be transported in one go through one means or another, not all of these methods are suitable for delivery to this area. Furthermore, of those transportation vessels managing to reach their drop-off

Kim Jong Un inspects SOF personnel undergoing a briefing. Their laptops display (commercial) satellite imagery of South Korea's Strategic Missile Command headquarters. (KCBC)

zone safely, many will have been compromised and run a very high risk of being targeted by South Korean forces on their way back. In fact, even if the bulk evaded detection as they crossed the border southward (by all means a highly unlikely eventuality), it is believed only a tiny portion would return successfully to stage a second wave. This would leave a large part of the roughly 60,000 dedicated SOF without a specialised means of transportation, relying instead on regular insertion methods over ground.

In the air, means of insertion are divided between the KPAAF's helicopter force and its fleet of An-2 biplanes and three Il-76TD cargo aircraft, the latter of which can be used to carry over 120 paratroopers each (although at least one aircraft is destined to become an AEW&C platform in the near future). The former of these – while also potentially used in the airmobile role for transporting units closer to the front line – would be especially important in enabling operations in the strategic rear as they can carry up to 12 paratroopers over large distances while maintaining low altitude and reducing the chances of detection. Although these aircraft were built with landings on unprepared airstrips or even open fields in mind, paradrops would be their primary method of employment, utilising the dozens of dirt landing strips scattered across the DPRK (yet concentrated in the half closest to the DMZ) to facilitate their operations. In the past, infiltration may have occurred through two or three concentrated masses of aircraft flying along the same routes; nowadays a more scattered approach appears to be favoured. Since large masses of aircraft would form easy prey for South Korean defences, with the KPAAF unlikely to be able to provide much protection, solitary aircraft each departing to their own destination are deemed to have a higher chance of success. The risk of losing their way during these insertions, which may well be conducted under the cover of night, is mitigated by newly installed GPS-devices and terrain-following radars. The latter is of importance considering that GPS can and would be subject to heavy jamming, while terrain-following radars aid not just with navigation but also with nap-of-the-earth flight which can be especially difficult over the forested and mountainous Korean Peninsula. Other propeller aircraft, such as the Yak-18, could be used to create diversions by dropping chaff and decoys in an attempt to draw away attention, though modern radars are generally well-equipped to identify such tactics. Light fire support is organic to the An-2 units, with many aircraft fitted with rocket pods, bombs or other specialised weaponry. Still, their complete lack of any ability to deal with opposing aircraft means their modus operandi would not deviate much from swift insertion and an immediate return to the North to increase chances of continued operation. There is also some indication that some North Korean SOF units have been trained to use paragliders for a stealthy insertion into the South, a tactic proven highly effective during Hamas's attack on Israel on 7 October 2023.[34] (Motorised) paragliders can be highly compact and easy to transport on foot, while forming a difficult target to detect and shoot down while airborne.

Helicopter forces are typically used over shorter ranges in combat zones, and although large numbers are available many would be used in the light attack role instead. Those reserved for insertion missions may be focussed on operations closer to the front lines, and would be used with other forces, such as the light infantry units, as well. The large numbers of MD-500s

SOF soldiers parachute from North Korea's two remaining Il-76 cargo aircraft (one of three having been converted into an airborne early warning and control role aircraft) in early 2024. Since these aircraft are relatively easy targets for enemy fighters and air-defence systems, such a scenario is likely to be limited to peacetime exercises. (KCBC)

Two North Korean paratroopers come in to land. Both are wielding Type-88 assault rifles with 'jungle-style' (taped) magazines. (KCBC)

Soldiers belonging to Unit 525 board a Mi-8 during the simulated Blue House raid in December 2016. (KCBC)

An MD-500E overflying SOF exercises simulating a Blue House raid in 2016. It was later used to extract a puppet representing a (South Korean) VIP. (KCBC)

imported in the late 1980s are technically capable of transporting two to six (the latter with four soldiers holding onto the outside of the helicopter) SOF, but would likely be used sparingly for transportation into combat zones. Still, as they are ideally suited for special operations, and were notably used for the extraction of a VIP during the simulated Blue House raid in 2016, it is certain they will see heavy use by the SOF. The fact that these aircraft are also operated by the ROKA means that they could be used to sow confusion amongst South Korean forces, aiding in SOF operations. However, modern communications systems between ROKA assets diminish the chances of this ruse succeeding, and as the MD-500 is slated for replacement in the coming decade it will soon cease to hold any significance in such a role. A more likely, albeit still unconventional, workhorse for helicopter insertions is the Soviet/Polish Mi-2, making up the bulk of the KPA's helicopter forces. Although they are light, up to eight SOF may be carried at a time, though possibly fewer with a heavy weapons load. The Mi-2s are joined by roughly 40 Mi-4/Z-5s, which while capable of carrying up to 16 SOF lack the speed and agility of the Mi-2, thus generally requiring a safer environment in order to operate successfully. The still larger Mi-8 offers far better flight characteristics, carrying up to 26 passengers over great distances at far greater speeds, nevertheless, the fact that far fewer helicopters of this type are available means they will have a relatively small impact on SOF insertion numbers. On the whole, perhaps 5,600 SOF could be inserted into the South by air in total, with sharply diminishing returns on each flight after the first.

The transportation situation is slightly better for the navy's two Sniper Brigades and three amphibious light infantry brigades, which would be mainly inserted by

North Korean paratroopers with each two F-7 rounds for the Type-68 RPG (left) and mortar rounds (right) crammed in between their bodies and gear. (KCBC)

The MD-500(E) is among the most numerous helicopters in KPAAF service, and together with the Mi-8 the only type thought to be used for SOF operations. Due to its compact size and agility, the MD-500 is well-suited for low-altitude incursions into South Korea, albeit with the drawback of being able to carry only a few armed SOF soldiers. It was suspected that North Korea painted some of its MD-500s in South Korean camouflage to deceive South Korean soldiers into mistaking them for their own helicopters. However, as South Korea moves towards phasing out the MD-500 in favour of modern replacements, this strategy will soon lose its effectiveness. (Artwork by Luca Canossa)

Although North Korea's Mi-8Ts are some of the oldest helicopters of their type still in service worldwide, they remain among the most capable helicopters within the country's fleet. While the majority function in an unarmed capacity, this particular model is among the few equipped with two stub wings, each carrying a total of six rocket pods of unknown calibre. Despite this modification, its infantry-carrying capabilities remain relatively unchanged, which is particularly advantageous given the scarcity of Mi-8s available. This Mi-8T features the newly introduced arid camouflage pattern which is being applied to a significant number of KPAAF helicopters, complementing the green pattern introduced in the mid-2010s. (Artwork by Luca Canossa)

Close to 300 An-2/Y-5 aircraft serve as the primary mode of transportation for the KPAAF's Sniper Brigades and SOF. With a capacity to transport over a dozen SOF soldiers, North Korea has pursued several upgrade programmes over the years to enhance the aircraft's capabilities. This has entailed the fitting of terrain-following radars, improvements to navigational and communications equipment and the incorporation of armament onto certain aircraft. During wartime, the An-2/Y-5 fleet is set to operate from numerous small dirt strips situated in close proximity to the DMZ. (Artwork by Tom Cooper)

the KPAN's fleet of up to 200 hovercraft, other light landing craft and inflatable dinghies. Divided amongst the Kong Bang II and Kong Bang III classes respectively capable of carrying some 50 and 40 personnel, the hovercraft force alone would be able to deploy up to 8,000 personnel. Since these rely on massed landings, evading Southern defences through sheer speed combined with the element of surprise, their use during a second landing attempt is thought to be even more limited than for aircraft attempting to invade through South Korean airspace. Even if they manage to make their way back into the North unharmed, after the initial landings the ROKA would be fully alerted and subsequent operations would be quickly curtailed. Over short distances, speedboats provide a stealthy but fast alternative, whereas other specialised infiltration craft and submarines could be used over larger distances but are likely to be used exclusively by the RGB. 'Human torpedo' submarines – a type of diver propulsion vehicle – would also be used in large numbers by the Maritime Sniper Brigades, with a total of some 32 indigenously-built 18-metre-long examples confirmed to exist. Though some have claimed that the use of these vehicles could be extended to suicide missions, whereby a diver actively guides a torpedo towards its target while riding it, it is more likely that they would operate solely to guide special operations or stealthy insertion missions.[35]

Famously, the DPRK inserted 120 SOF commandos by seaborne infiltration on South Korea's east coast on 30 October 1968 with the objective of utilising the mountainous east coast as a staging ground for a revolutionary army comprised of Southerners to oust the regime of Park Chung Hee. North Korea had greatly overestimated the South Korean citizens' will to do so however, and security forces were soon alerted to the presence of large numbers of North Korean soldiers in the Taebaek Mountains.[36] As the former launched a large-scale operation aimed at neutralising the threat, the North Korean SOF were battling for their lives as opposed to enticing the local population to revolt against the government. Perhaps unsurprisingly, the landings ended in spectacular failure when most of the North Korean commandos were killed or captured by December 1968.

Thirteen thousand SOF personnel delivered in a first wave at various places near or in the ROK's strategic rear is an impressive figure, but it falls far short of the numbers required to create a literal second front. Instead of actually capturing or destroying well-defended army assets, the SOF would serve to draw away resources, with such instances as the 1996 Gangneung submarine infiltration alone sparking a massive manhunt. Since regular ROKA units would be mostly engaged near the regular front along the DMZ, the ensuing chaos would require the mobilisation of the Homeland Reserve Forces, which are more prone to suffer from a lack of training and poor equipment. The many uncertainties in the

Soldiers from one of the navy's two Sniper Brigades wield the latest version of the Type-88 rifle. Also note the inflatable life jackets and boonie hats, possibly influenced by the attire of the US Navy SEALS. (KCBC)

Small craft like these are ideal for covert infiltration of islands along the Northern Limit Line. The combat swimmers on board are equipped with a combination of Type-88 carbines and bolt-action light grenade launchers. (KCBC)

Kong Bang II and Kong Bang III hovercraft belonging to the KPAN conduct an amphibious assault exercise. (KCBC)

SOF soldiers emerge from a Kong Bang II hovercraft carrying spades. (KCBC)

strategic SOF's operational methods and their efficacy means they represent perhaps the greatest wild card of all those assets available to the KPA, having the potential to completely destabilise ROKA operations in the rear while at the same time risking abject failure in the very opening stages of a war.

While technically distinct from the SOF, units affiliated with the Ministry of State Security and Ministry of Social Security can also be regarded as elite. They are slated to undertake similar duties to the SOF during wartime and have been witnessed participating in exercises alongside SOF units, such as the simulated storming of a South Korean DMZ guard post. Another crucial wartime objective would involve thwarting infiltrations by ROK or US special forces and to secure the rear of the DPRK. In pursuit of these mission objectives, the Ministry of Social Security has at its disposal a variety of conventional weapons systems, including 6x6 M-2010 armoured personnel carriers. Furthermore, its troops are among the foremost to receive newly issued weaponry and equipment. This has entailed upgraded versions of the Type-88 assault rifles equipped with helical magazines and suppressors. Troops belonging to the Ministry of Social Security are easily recognised by their distinct black uniforms and black helmets complete with visors.

Another notable elite unit separate from the SOF is the Guard Command, which is responsible for the protection of the Kim family as well as other VIPs such as high-ranking party members and officials. It provides anything from (uniformed or incognito) bodyguards for personal protection to entire guard units for securing important facilities and houses. The Guard Command also boasts significant conventional military assets to enable it some resistance against any coup attempts by well-equipped army units, in which capacity it works closely together with the 91 Capital Defence Corps and forces of the Ministry of State Security and Ministry of Social Security. Its forerunner was established in 1946, yet it has seen several changes since this first incarnation, not least during power shifts such as witnessed in the early 1990s when Kim Jong Il took over.[37] In restructuring the Guard Command, Kim Jong Il most notably established Unit 2.16 (referring to his own birthday) for his personal protection. After Kim Jong Un rose to power, it is likely that he followed in his father's footsteps and created a similar unit on the foundations of the old one. As the Guard Command reports directly to Kim Jong Un, this would be his most trusted and valued organisation. In this capacity, it is perhaps best known for providing his personal protection during his inspections of the nation. As these visits are typically broadcast as part of state propaganda, these bodyguards are frequently seen despite their best efforts to avoid the cameras. They were also the first to be issued new Type-88 assault rifles that sported distinctive helical magazines, allowing each guard to fire roughly 150 shots before having to reload – with two additional magazines being carried providing a significant supply of ammunition. This would be ideally suited for dealing with large and potentially hostile crowds, or a prolonged fire fight which might occur during an ambush. That threats to North Korea's leadership might also come from outside the country was attested by a botched submarine infiltration operation carried out by US special forces in 2019. The intended goal was to plant listening devices to intercept the communications of Kim Jong Un, amid nuclear talks with President Trump. The mission went awry long before the Guard Command could ever have come in however. After the team encountered a small fishing boat, they reportedly killed the crew to prevent them from alerting authorities, and then aborted the mission.[38]

Uniformed personnel from the Ministry of State Security march in formation during a parade. (KCBC)

Troops belonging to the Ministry of Social Security engage in a live-fire exercise in March 2024 with Kim Jong Un in attendance. Their distinctive black uniforms make them easily identifiable. (KCBC)

A North Korean SOF soldier aims down the sight of the 'NK11' multi-weapon. Equipped with whatever best equipment can be obtained, he wears a flak jacket donning a digital camouflage pattern and has a night-vision goggles mount on his helmet, which is modelled after the popular US PASGT series of helmets. Nonetheless, this equipment pales in comparison to the size and stature of his bullpup dual-barrel multi-weapon, which greatly increases the range of targets that can be engaged and dealt with. (Artwork by Adam Hook)

As the DPRK's foremost tool for conducting asymmetrical warfare, its special operations forces remain one of the most difficult to assess. Perhaps precisely for this reason, it ranks amongst the most highly valued in the North's military, receiving the best human and technological resources and regularly featuring in its defence posturing. In this role it constitutes somewhat of a wildcard in terms of its potential impact on a renewed conflict with the South, with no true equivalent abroad against which to gauge its abilities. With so many uncertainties surrounding this fifth spoke of the KPA's military wheel, it bears similarity to perhaps the biggest wildcard of all in North Korea's military: its strategic deterrent.

A SOF paratrooper armed with a Type-88-derived carbine stands ready to board the aircraft that will take him to his designated drop zone. He is heavily packed with parachutes and additional gear such as ammunition, explosives and mission-specific equipment in a dedicated carry-on bag. Unlikely to be resupplied while operating far behind enemy lines, much of his North Korean gear will likely make way for ROKA weapons and equipment the longer his stay in the rear of the ROK endures. Also note the night-vision goggles installed on his new-issue helmet. (Artwork by Adam Hook)

A member of the Guard Command stands guard holding a Type-88 with top-folding stock and high-capacity helical magazine. Tasked with the personal protection of the Kim family and other high-ranking officials, members of the Guard Command are generally disliked for their aggressive attitude towards other soldiers and crowds during visits of the Supreme Leader. In this role they are known to push, punch and even hit people with the end of their buttstock for coming too close to the Leader. In the case crowds would suddenly turn hostile, each guard has about 150 rounds ready to fire, with two spare magazines carried in pouches on his back allowing him to fire another 300 rounds in rapid succession. (Artwork by Adam Hook)

CHAPTER 2

MISSILE GENERAL BUREAU

Undoubtedly the most vaunted and feared branch of the North Korean military is its Missile General Bureau (MGB). As the primary delivery system for weapons of mass destruction (WMDs), the international focus on ballistic missiles is understandable, and the North's exhaustive investment in this area should be of considerable concern. Still, intelligence on the MGB has been contradictory at best, and misinformation is rampant both on its history and current composition. The lack of an oversight of strategic weaponry available to the DPRK means that its capabilities are difficult to assess, which can seriously impede accurate policymaking. Furthermore, without an accurate reading of its history future developments will always come as a surprise – which is the key element the MGB has banked on for its unexpected successes in recent years. As one of the youngest branches of the KPA and notably the one prioritised in Kim Jong Un's Pyongjin Line policy, which seeks the simultaneous development of the economy and nuclear weapons, it has undergone the largest technological and numerical upheaval of all branches in the past few years. New designs have been tested at unprecedented rates not only for North Korean standards but for any nation researching ballistic missile related technologies in history. The Pyongjin Line itself materialised in an uncannily fast push for public proof that the DPRK's nuclear deterrent is fully operational, which was achieved through uncommonly transparent coverage of practically every step required along the way. This culminated with tests of precision-guided payloads, submarine-launched ballistic missiles and as its *pièce de résistance* road-mobile intercontinental ballistic missiles capable of targeting the entire US mainland, and with it, much of the globe. Its successes have come with advances in the DPRK's WMD programmes and particularly nuclear weapons research, and were inevitably paired with soaring tensions on the Korean Peninsula. With its key role in the past, present and especially future of not only the immediate region but quite possibly the entire world, the MGB is perhaps the single most important branch of the KPA, and correspondingly one of the most secretive.

Unsurprisingly, very little is known about the MGB organisationally. The DPRK's missile forces were first grouped under the Missile/Artillery Guidance Bureau, which was renamed to the Strategic Rocket Force on 3 July 1999, now celebrated as the Day of the Strategic Force, becoming an independent service alongside the other branches of the KPA.[1] Nevertheless, only in March 2012 did this reorganisation become apparent – telling of the secrecy surrounding this branch. In the early 2020s, a further reorganisation saw the branch renamed yet again to the Missile General Bureau, possibly to reflect the fact it supervises the potential use of the DPRK's tactical nuclear arsenal through a large variety of delivery systems as well. Nevertheless, its exact structure, as well as what weapons systems precisely are its purview remains largely a mystery. What is known is that at least 13 strategic missile brigades exist subordinate to the MGB, each of undetermined size and composition. Although certain artillery rockets and tactical ballistic missiles might also be used by KPAGF units, even within the MGB itself there is significant overlap in mission scope for each system, with a variety of weaponry capable of tackling the same task should the requirement arise. Since, in keeping with KPA doctrine, no successful systems are ever truly retired (with the possible exception of its very oldest generation of artillery rockets), especially for shorter ranges and light payloads a multitude of both older and newer ballistic missiles coexist in the same role, albeit with differing efficacy. The resulting complexity can be difficult to analyse properly, and the fact that North Korea is outputting new indigenous missile designs at an unprecedented rate means that missile launch types are frequently misidentified. Although in the media and official statements an emphasis is usually placed on such new long-ranged systems that may, for instance, grant the DPRK the ability to strike the US mainland with a nuclear weapon, the impact of new shorter-ranged systems is mostly overlooked. These systems are much more likely to see successful deployment during a conflict on the Korean Peninsula, taking over some of the tasks that may traditionally be carried by the air force, aside from forming a potent deterrent. Such military bases as Camp Humphreys, currently the US's largest overseas military garrison, are well within reach of short-ranged ballistic missiles and will attract massive volumes of fire from the onset of hostilities. Within the DPRK's immediate region, ballistic missiles can be used in similar fashion targeting South Korean, Japanese and US military bases, airfields and ports as far as Guam. In this role WMDs can be used to vastly increase their efficacy, although obviously at the risk of disproportionate retaliation. While WMDs can be deployed by nearly all of the KPA's branches, the MGB is of especially great importance in this regard and the DPRK's WMD programmes are therefore briefly treated in this volume. Similarly, the MGB has had offshoots in the form of an indigenous space programme often tied to its missile programme, which although falling under the National Aerospace Technology Administration is best placed in the context of its technological origins: the MGB.

Programme Origins

Although North Korea's missile programme is often stated to have commenced with the acquisition of R-17 Elbrus 'Scud-B' tactical ballistic missiles during the 1980s, North Korea itself appears to use a different system of classifications and as such claims it started in the late 1960s. This entailed copying and manufacturing Soviet artillery rockets under the designation 'Hwasong' (the Korean name for the planet Mars), although details surrounding these first attempts at producing tactical rocket systems remain murky. For instance, it is unclear exactly to which system the Hwasong-1 refers, although a likely candidate is the 2K6 Luna 'FROG-3' artillery rocket system, which was delivered alongside the 9K52 Luna-M 'FROG-7' in the 1960s.[2] The 2K6 was copied on the basis of a Sungri No.2 truck, providing the KPA with an early indigenous long-ranged artillery rocket asset. Establishing production of artillery rockets in the early 1970s was an unprecedented achievement, and it illustrates just how soon long-ranged assets came to be valued in the KPA. The Luna-M was also claimed to have been copied as the Hwasong-3 in the early 1970s, although this appears to have been a mixed success, with some reports stating production ceased shortly after.[3] [4] It is uncertain if the associated 9P113 transporter erector launcher (TEL) was ever produced, with a modern 300mm MRL system using a truck cannibalised (or derived) from the Luna-M's, suggesting the

Top left: A rare photograph of a North Korean 2K6 Luna 'FROG-3' artillery rocket system. Combining a circular error probable (CEP) of just under a kilometre with an equally unimpressive range that only just outmatches that of the 170mm Koksan SPG (without rocket assisted projectiles), the system's relatively heavy warhead likely is the only redeeming factor that allowed its continued active service into the twenty-first century. (KCBC)

Top right: The presumed Hwasong-1 (a variant of the 2K6 Luna on a Sungri No.2 truck), starting point of North Korea's ballistic missile ventures, during a parade in 1972. (KCBC)

Left: North Korean Hwasong-3/FROG-7s parading through Pyongyang during the celebration of the 80th anniversary of Kim Il Sung's birthday in 1992. The introduction of a new 300mm MRL that seems to utilise a modified ZIL-135 chassis means that their status is now uncertain, and presumed retired. (KCBC)

Luna-M and its copies might now be retired. Even less is known about the inferred Hwasong-2 and Hwasong-4, which never reached production.

However, one possibility is that the Hwasong-4 designation refers to a short-lived joint project between the People's Republic of China (PRC) and the DPRK in the late 1970s, which called for the development of a short-range ballistic missile (SRBM) publicly known as the DF-61.[5] The programme, which hoped to achieve the introduction of a liquid-fuelled mobile missile system with a maximum range of some 600 kilometres and a payload of 1,000 kilogrammes, was reportedly launched in response to Soviet reluctance to deliver modern ballistic missile systems to North Korea during the downturn in relations of the late 1970s and early 1980s.[6] After the main backer of the project from the Chinese side, Chen Xilian, was purged at the end of the 1970s, the programme apparently died off, but not without providing North Korean missile engineers with a wealth of knowledge about indigenously producing such systems.

To the North Korean military, the real success story started in the 1980s with the copying of the infamous Soviet R-17E 'Scud-B' SRBM. Despite the extremely prolific production of this system and its derivatives, and subsequent exports that garnered significant international attention to the North Korean ballistic missile programme, the origin story of how they acquired the system remains a subject of debate. The prevalent theory suggests North Korea turned to Egypt as a source for the system after the Soviet Union refused to provide it, which delivered a number of missiles and at least one MAZ-543 TEL for study as a result. This theory is supported by a multitude of reports claiming prior cooperation with copying the 9K52 Luna-M, and continued arms deals struck during the 1980s and 1990s stemming from a history of close military cooperation.[7] When the Scuds were delivered according to this theory is also subject to some ambiguity, as some sources claim they first arrived during 1976 and others 1981.[8] While the delivery of Scuds from Egypt is plausible, nowadays the theory is often discredited due to evidence implying extensive Soviet aid in the setting up of its ballistic missile industry, thus negating the need for a secondary supplier of the system. In reality, a mixture of both theories is likely to come closest to the truth, with Egypt providing some of the missiles it received in 1973 thus setting off the DPRK's programme, which only gained the Soviet Union's support after relations thawed in the mid-1980s. Regardless, it is certain that North Korea managed to produce its first working copy and test it successfully in 1984, receiving the designation of Hwasong-5 and swiftly entering mass production.[9] Interestingly, there is evidence to suggest that North Korea initially faced difficulty in copying the MAZ-543 TEL and thus based its prototypes on trailers and makeshift TELs instead, a solution also employed by other nations which faced the same problem, such as Iran and Iraq. Nonetheless, it seems these problems were relatively short lived, and by 1985 the first deal for exporting both missiles and TELs to Iran had been closed, with deliveries starting in 1987. This included both indigenously-built TELs which differ from the regular MAZ-543 usually seen in some minor details, and some that used an imported Japanese 8x8 Nissan chassis, copied by Iran as the Khaybar-25. Tellingly, most subsequent deals, often closed with nations already in possession of the R-17, would omit the launching vehicle, making it likely Iran is the only other nation to operate North Korean-built MAZ-543 and 8x8 Nissan TELs. In 1993 US intelligence officials also indicated that the DPRK had imported vehicles from Germany's MAN truck company for use as ballistic missile TELs, further underlining the difficulties North Korea was facing producing its own launch platforms. North Korean export brochures later depicted a hybrid MAN KAT 1/MAZ-543 TEL in use with a foreign nation, thought to be either the UAE or Saudi Arabia.[10]

An alternative theory on the origin of the Hwasong-5 comes from a North Korean defector which claims 20 R-17E were delivered by the Soviet Union in 1972 in exchange for the intelligence contained aboard the USS *Pueblo*, which was captured by North Korea in early 1968.[11] While the gap between delivery and indigenous manufacture

Kim Jong Il inspecting a possibly Egyptian-sourced 8K14E (R-17E) missile in the early 1980s. (KCBC)

A North Korean Hwasong-5 missile is launched from its TEL during a March 2016 exercise. (KCBC)

A North Korean 8x8 Nissan TEL in Iranian service. (ACIG via IRIB)

An early North Korean Hwasong-5 on the basis of a hybrid MAN KAT 1/MAZ-543 TEL. The same image was used to advertise North Korean Scuds on the website of notorious arms dealer Jean-Bernard Lasnaud at the start of the 2000s. (Wingman Media)

of the system could be explained by the technological difficulties in accomplishing such a feat, no tests of the R-17E were reported during the 1970s and early 1980s either, therefore making this theory implausible. Still, reports of Soviet assistance in the North Korean missile programme are plentiful, and it is indeed likely that after a strengthening of ties during the 1980s the Soviet Union agreed to cooperate after all.

Whether this was the case or not, developments later proceeded at an impressive rate and after reported experiments aimed at drastically reducing the CEP of the Hwasong-5 in 1987, the Hwasong-6 SRBM was first tested in 1988, which is often referred to in the West as the 'Scud-C'.[12] This designation is problematic to say the least; not only is it confusing as the Hwasong-6 is an indigenous North Korean product, it is also contradictory as the moniker 'Scud-C' had already been assigned to a Soviet extended-range prototype of the Scud-B. The confusion is further exacerbated by alleged technological ties of the Soviet missile to the Hwasong-6. As it happens, North Korea appears to market many of its ballistic missiles abroad as various types of 'Scud' missiles, even when the type does not have any relation to this design, with Scud-B referring to the Hwasong-5 and Scud-C to the Hwasong-6. The Hwasong-6, which is outwardly almost indistinguishable from the Hwasong-5 and is in fact fired from the same TEL, offers a significantly increased maximum range of some 500 kilometres. This was achieved partly by redesigning a section of the guidance suite, allowing for the fuel and oxidiser tanks to be extended.[13] Additionally, the Hwasong-6 carries a warhead of roughly 750 kilogrammes as opposed to that of the Hwasong-5 which weighs close to a tonne.[14] Perhaps more importantly however, North Korean sources claim the Hwasong-6 can be equipped with a new guidance system which allows it to reduce the Hwasong-5's CEP of around half a kilometre to just 50 metres, thereby greatly enhancing the effectiveness of the missile when used in a conventional role.[15] Export brochures dated to January 2017 would later unveil that special cluster and thermobaric warheads were developed for the system, which was marketed at exorbitant prices for its antiquated characteristics.[16]

Having truly kicked off its indigenous ballistic missile industry, North Korea set out to become a major exporter of these technologies, providing them to half a dozen other nations in the following decades. These included reported deliveries of Hwasong-5s and/or Hwasong-6s to Egypt, Libya, Pakistan, Syria, the UAE, Vietnam and Yemen. Their age, questionable quality, general obsoleteness and political unpalatability means not many of these are still in use with these nations today, but Hwasong missiles have spurred on indigenous ballistic missile programmes in several of these nations and were even fired at Saudi Arabia during the Saudi Arabian-led intervention in Yemen. These deliveries caused great concern for further proliferation of sensitive technologies by the DPRK, and for the first time focussed international attention on the clandestine exports of this comparatively tiny nation. Nevertheless, North Korea steamed ahead with its investments in this field, and in the 1980s and 1990s began purchasing from abroad and

The rear end of one of 15 Hwasong-5/6 missiles that were discovered hidden under sacks of cement aboard the North Korean freighter *So San* in 2002. Intercepted on its way to Yemen, the intended recipient of the missiles, the vessel was allowed to continue its journey after inspection by the US Navy. It is presumed that at least some of these missiles were later fired at Saudi Arabia by Houthi rebels. (United States Navy)

A neatly camouflaged Hwasong-5/6 missile photographed by a member of a Myanmarese delegation during a tour of one of North Korea's underground missile factories in 2008. Despite an apparent genuine interest in acquiring such hardware from North Korea, Myanmar eventually refrained from pursuing a ballistic missile programme of its own. (Authors' archive)

eventually indigenously producing so-called Computer Numerical Control (CNC) machines. These sophisticated devices are capable of producing delicate components usable in ballistic missiles or other complex devices, and thus decrease North Korean reliance on foreign acquisitions. Since beginning their production in 1995 CNC machines have occupied an increasingly prominent role in the DPRK's state propaganda, and by 2017 it operated as many as 15,000 examples for use in modern armament production.[17]

Liquid-Fuelled Ballistic Missiles

As it was by far the most prolifically produced ballistic missile system in use with North Korea, the Hwasong-6 would form the mainstay of its strategic forces for decades, and even be reincarnated in a far more advanced Hwasong variant in the 2010s. This system, the Hwasong designation of which is unknown (US Department of Defense (DoD) designation KN-10 and/or KN-18), was unveiled during the 2017 parade for the 105th anniversary of Kim Il Sung's birthday, and the first publicised test took place shortly thereafter in late May. Modifications to the missile itself are relatively modest, yet highly significant in the increase in capabilities they offer. By far the most noticeable aspect is its new tracked TEL, an offspring of North Korea's tank industry that was likely necessitated by the fact that the regular wheeled MAZ-543-derived TELs were much more complicated to produce, and possibly required components to be imported from abroad. Interestingly, the original R-11M missile that initiated the Scud family used a very similar looking TEL also based on a heavy tank chassis, which was foregone when Soviet leader Nikita Khrushchev halted the production of the Soviet Union's heavy tank lines, a not unwelcome decision as it introduced vibrations that upset the missile's sensitive electronics.[18] Despite its potential drawbacks, the new tracked TEL has the advantage that it is capable of traversing rougher terrain than the MAZ-543, thus increasing the amount of possible launch locations. Also, the Korean Central News Agency (KCNA) press release covering the first test launch hinted that its instrument panels had been improved, thereby further automating the pre-launch preparations and reducing launch time.[19] US intelligence statements further suggest that the system unlike the earlier Hwasong-5 and Hwasong-6 utilises a separating warhead, presumably to aid with guidance in the final approach. Confusingly, three ballistic missiles reported to have been launched on 26 August the same year also utilised technologies introduced on the Hwasong-6 reincarnation, but were assessed to have been based on Hwasong-5 missiles with non-separating warheads (receiving the US DoD designation of KN-21).[20] Whether this intelligence is accurate is questionable, and North Korea did not disclose any details about the tests, which could well have been of one of the variety of other new missile systems later unveiled instead.

Several KN-18 TELs pass by during the 105th anniversary of Kim Il Sung's birthday parade of 2017. In a highly unconventional move North Korea forwent the regular MAZ-543 wheeled chassis and used a tracked chassis instead. Although this has the potential to negatively impact internal components of the missile, it allows the MGB to produce more TELs than it would have with a wheeled chassis. (NK Pro)

Aside from the system's new TEL, which could presumably also be used in conjunction with the Hwasong-5 and 6, the missile itself also sports an important innovation. Its regular, inertially guided warhead has been traded for a so-called Manoeuvrable Re-entry Vehicle (MaRV), which adjusts its flight trajectory in the mid and terminal flight sections in order to achieve a much higher accuracy, additionally making it much harder to shoot down by interrupting its predictable ballistic path. Footage of a programme that allegedly showed the missile's flight telemetry asserts that it hit a simulated target at 450 kilometres distance with just seven metres of deviation. Of course, only the former could be verified by external measurements of the missile's trajectory, but the reported accuracy is not uncommon for a MaRV design. To accommodate the warhead's guidance mechanisms, its weight was increased, thus slightly limiting its range to around 450 kilometres. Trajectory adjustments are executed during the missile's first stage of flight through four flaps fitted to the nose cone, and later by a small engine fitted below the warhead. To explain why North Korea had gone to such length to design a new Hwasong-6 derivative with a MaRV warhead, it was initially suspected the missile might be employed as an anti-ship ballistic missile (ASBM), which potentially form a very effective deterrent to large naval craft. In such capacity its long range, heavy warhead and high velocity of more than Mach 5 would allow it to be used even as a 'carrier killer', complicating the deployment of US aircraft carriers in the region. However, various aspects point towards the fact that this is not the case. Most importantly, as of yet it appears the KN-18 uses global navigation satellite system (GNSS) guidance instead of the optical or passive/active radar guidance usually required for an ASBM, which makes it unsuitable for use against any moving target as it will long have moved on from the chosen coordinates by the time the missile arrives. However, even with appropriate guidance an ASBM is only truly effective when it is backed up by a sophisticated network of detection systems. In the case of North Korea, this would have to consist of coastal defence radars and reconnaissance aircraft/UAVs (barring the development of more sophisticated reconnaissance satellites), both of which are highly vulnerable to the weaponry a typical carrier group will bring with it. An effective ASBM system would therefore require a missile system with much shorter response time, improved guidance methods, and a network of potent detection systems for support: a prospect that in 2017 could only be considered a very distant threat.

A KN-18 missile is launched from its TEL during the sole publicised test on 28 May 2017. (KCBC)

Nonetheless, the introduction of this system for the first time gave North Korea the ability to strike any hardened target in most of South Korea with pinpoint accuracy at a relatively low cost, gravely endangering military bases and airfields that might have been missed by a wide margin in earlier systems. The use of ballistic missile defence systems such as the Terminal High Altitude Area Defense (THAAD) to counter this threat is also countered not only by the large volume of missiles likely to be launched during a war, not all of which would have to be guided, but also because warheads capable of terminal manoeuvring are notoriously difficult to shoot down. Some three decades after the DPRK first began to introduce its very own ballistic missile technologies, from their fully matured offshoots a very clear picture began to arise of where their future ambitions lay. Just half a decade later again, North Korea's strategic landscape would be virtually unrecognisable.

Back to the previous century, during which North Korea's ambitions soon outgrew the restrictive R-17 design, and a much more radical conversion, receiving the moniker 'Nodong-1' in the West, underwent preliminary tests in the early 1990s before achieving its maiden flight in 1992.[21] Designated the Hwasong-7, this system uses a missile that was large enough to warrant the development of a new lengthened TEL based on the MAZ-543. This was done by adding a single axle to the rear of the vehicle, thereby increasing its length by some two metres, and redesigning the erection mechanism to cope with the increased size. However, this additional axle is not engine driven and the vehicle still seems to use the original engine associated with the MAZ-543, and as such the resulting 10x8 vehicle can be expected to have diminished performance. It appears that at a later date small numbers of an upgraded variant which does provide drive for its rear axle were produced, but due to the complexity of these 10x10 vehicles they remain a rare sight. Two different missiles are known to be used by this system, both of which resemble scaled up variants of the original R-17, measuring some 1.35 metres in diameter and 15 metres in length. Their most apparent difference is in the size of the warhead: while one variant uses a regular conical nose cone capable of containing a warhead weighing some 1,000 kilogrammes, the other employs a lighter 'triconic' nose cone which can carry a warhead weighing some 700 kilogrammes, thus extending the system's range substantially. The Hwasong-7 has historically been restricted in its testing due to the proximity of foreign aerospace and limited space available however, and it is presumed that this is the main reason why tests are often conducted at a very high angle, due to which the missiles attain a much higher altitude but also a much shorter range. Nonetheless, at least one of each missile variant has been tested in a foreign country to a range of no less than 1,000 kilometres, landing it conclusively in the medium-range ballistic missile (MRBM) category and putting most of Japan within range.[22] Unfortunately, what scarce footage of North Korean Hwasong-7 tests exists has never been tied to a particular missile trajectory, so it is uncertain which variant is capable of attaining which range. However, comparison with the Iranian Shahab-3A and B missile variants, thought to be direct copies of the North Korean designs, suggest a possible maximum range of some 1,280 kilometres for the 1,000 kilogramme variant, and up to 1,930 kilometres for the lighter variant.[23] The increase in missile size, the redesign of the body, to the point of swapping the places of the fuel and oxidiser tanks, and especially the upscaling of its engine was impressive at this stage in the DPRK's missile programme, and the fact that certain engineering solutions appear to predate the R-17's design suggest Soviet aid was instrumental to its development.[24] The missile is marketed abroad as the Scud-E, variously said to be capable of attaining 1,350 and 1,500

The first Hwasong-7 variant employs a conical nose cone similar to that of the R-17 missile employed by the Scud system. Rarely sighted since its inception in the early 1990s, the conical nose cone was supplemented by a variant with a triconic nose cone carrying a lighter warhead allowing for increased range. (KCBC)

Hwasong-7 missiles on their TELs are paraded through Pyongyang during the 60th anniversary of the Korean War armistice parade in 2013. (KCBC)

kilometres in range without specifying which of the variants this entails.[25] For the former range, thermobaric and cluster warheads are available for export aside from the more conventional HE warhead, thus offering much greater effect on target for the same weight.[26] Notably, aside from Iran it seems Pakistan also benefited from exported Hwasong-7 technology, and both the Ghauri-I and later Ghauri-II seem to have been closely derived from it.

The Hwasong-8 designation was apparently reserved for an unknown missile that appears not to have entered service in the North Korean military. However, it is believed this designation refers to a missile supposedly offered for export as the Scud-D, and interest in this missile due to its alleged, but unconfirmed, export to nations such as Syria has led to a relatively accurate image of what it should constitute. As an evolutionary development of the Hwasong-6, it provides yet another range extension without swapping the engine or fuel and oxidiser types used, this time launching a warhead weighing some 500 kilogrammes to roughly 700 kilometres in distance. For this purpose, the instrument panel was rearranged and length of the body of the missile increased to roughly 12.4 metres to make space for longer fuel and oxidiser tanks.[27] Additionally, the fuel and oxidiser tanks are believed to have switched places in the missile body, mirroring developments in the Hwasong-7 and later Hwasong-9. Although it is believed to have been tested in Syria in September 2000, no Hwasong-8s have ever been spotted abroad, and the reason they did not enter service in the DPRK is unknown.[28] However, it may be because of the almost simultaneous development of the comparable but more modern and capable Hwasong-9, which can be thought of as the design that maximised the potential of the original 9D21 engine of the R-17.

This missile, yet another advanced Scud-based design of the 1990s that has remained largely unknown to the intelligence community until a test was covered by KCNA in July 2016, was supposedly first tested successfully in 1994, over two decades before its public debut.[29] The Hwasong-9 is the last missile in North Korea's arsenal that can be said to have been directly derived from the R-17, at least until the advent of the KN-10/KN-18 in the 2010s, and in fact still bears more resemblance to the original design than the Hwasong-7 does, despite incorporating several more advanced design elements.[30] Returning to a slightly modified variant of the indigenously produced 8x8 MAZ-543 TEL, the missile involved appears to have retained its R-17 legacy engine but is increased in diameter to a little over one metre, and in length to some 12.8 metres. It combines this with a 500 kilogramme warhead housed in a rearranged, 'biconic' nose cone and is speculated to use an aluminium tank structure in order to squeeze a 1,000 kilometre range out of this design, making it of comparable range to the 1,000 kilogramme warhead variant of the Hwasong-7 but presumably cheaper and easier to produce.[31] Although no specifics about its guidance systems are known, it presumably also benefited from the claimed CEP reductions also found on the Hwasong-6. As an export product, its long range and commonality with the MAZ-543 TEL would certainly make it attractive, but although longer-ranged Hwasong missiles have often been reported abroad, it does not appear a deal for the Hwasong-9 was ever struck. Nonetheless, a rare but very similar variant of the Iranian Shahab-3 missile indicates that a technology transfer may have occurred at some point.

The swift advances made during the mere decade it took to develop the Hwasong-5, -6, -7 and -9 are impressive for a nation like the DPRK to say the least, and it is likely some degree of Soviet/Russian assistance in these projects was responsible for their fast progression. Still, although R-17-derived designs set the stage for North Korea's entry to the world of strategic weaponry, an entirely new design would be required to allow it to start working towards its long-term ambitions of projecting its power on a much larger scale. The first missile that can be said to be in the intermediate-range ballistic missile (IRBM) class came in the form of the Hwasong-10, an ambitious new missile design that made waves in the West after it was revealed during the 65th anniversary of the foundation of the Workers' Party of Korea in 2010, receiving a variety of monikers such as 'Nodong-2', 'Nodong-B', 'Taepodong-X', 'Musudan' (after the missile test site at Musudan Ri) and 'BM-25' (often used when discussing supposed exports of the system, presumably meaning Ballistic Missile 25 – other North Korean export names are similarly unimaginative). The development of this missile can be described as rocky at best, and although it can be said to only have reached some form of operational stage after mid-2016, its origins trace all the way back to the 1990s. During this period, reports surfaced of Russian missile engineers and scientists being brought to the DPRK to assist in the development of a new type of missile. It appears the DPRK attempted to exploit the chaos created by the fall of the Soviet Union and thus import valuable knowledge without Russia's consent, a theory supported by the fact that throughout 1992 scores of Russian scientist were either stopped or even detained after trying to travel to North Korea.[32] Reports indicate that such efforts continued throughout the early 1990s, and although they failed several times it appears highly likely much of the technology used in the Hwasong-10 was acquired in this manner.[33] Tellingly, the Hwasong-10 is carried by a TEL that is clearly based on the Soviet MAZ-547W 12x12 truck also used for the Soviet RDS-10 IRBM, albeit with various modifications such as the addition of a launch

Four Hwasong-9 missiles are seen to be simultaneously launched from their TELs on 6 March 2017. Analysis has shown a possible fifth missile to have been involved in the exercise as well, but as it reportedly failed not long after launch it was excluded from state footage. (KCBC)

cabin in the middle of its body and another cabin on the upper right of the driver's cabin. These modifications, combined with the fact that importing these TELs from Belarus, where they would ordinarily be produced, would be difficult to conceal due to their size, indicate that North Korea manufactures and/or assembles these imposing vehicles indigenously, if only in limited numbers.[34]

The missile itself also bears heavy resemblance to the Soviet R-27(U) submarine-launched ballistic missile (SLBM), albeit while featuring a range of modifications to suit North Korea's needs. Most notably, its length has been increased from some 8.8 metres to roughly 11 metres, owing to the fact that the size of the fuel and oxidiser tanks has been increased.[35] The use of the R-27 as a basis for its design is significant not only because it grants the DPRK access to an entirely new engine and launch design, but also because its hypergolic propellant differs from that used in the R-17 series.[36] For one, the fuel component consists of the higher performing UDMH instead of the TM-185 used previously, enabling its use in later ballistic missile designs as well.[37] [38] However, the degree to which the new fuel impacts the Hwasong-10 actually depends on the exact oxidiser used in their design. The original R-27 used AK-27P inhibited red fuming nitric acid (IRFNA), similar to the AK-27I used for the R-17, but this was exchanged for the more potent N2O4/NTO on the R-27U, which together with an upgraded engine allowed it to attain a range of some 3,000 kilometres. Whether North Korea opted to stick to the AK-27P mixture or the much more pure and potent NTO is the subject of much debate, carrying implications not only for the Hwasong-10 but also for the capabilities of later North Korean liquid-fuelled ballistic missile designs. Although NTO is potentially capable of squeezing more range out of a missile, it is even more difficult to handle than the already extremely volatile and toxic IRFNA, and is therefore usually shunned in land-based mobile ballistic missiles. For one, NTO, or the alternative MON, has a very narrow range of temperatures at which it is liquid and thus suitable as an oxidiser, meaning any missile that makes use of it would require strict environmental control. Despite these severe drawbacks, simulations suggest NTO is a good match for a trajectory claimed for the missile in June 2016 by North Korea, even though the range gained by this decision still does not appear to allow it to reach further than 3,000 kilometres. At a distance of over 3,300 kilometres, this makes the often-mentioned target of the US military base on Guam out of reach for the Hwasong-10, even if a light warhead was used. Paradoxically, this means that even though the Hwasong-10 introduces a range of new technologies that are highly valuable to the DPRK's missile programme, it actually does little to amplify existing capabilities.

Despite the abundance of reports about Russian scientists collaborating on the development of the Hwasong-10 during the 1990s, it is only in the early 2000s that the first prototypes came into being, as is witnessed by an example bearing a commemoration plate of an inspection by Kim Jong Il in 2004. Still, no test launches were ever performed, prompting speculation that the ominous missiles first paraded in 2010 were in fact mock-ups representing a fake system, or that the missiles had been clandestinely tested in Iran instead. These speculations were put to rest after a sudden spate of testing in mid-2016, featuring at least six launches of which the last two were hailed as a success by North Korea. Nonetheless, the ROK Ministry of Defence (MoD) recognises eight tests in this period of which just one was deemed partially successful.[39] The explorative nature of the testing and differences between the tested missile and paraded examples, such as the addition of grid fins for in-flight stability, suggest that the system was indeed not fully operational prior to 2016. The long waiting time between initial development and actual testing may have been the result of the lack of funds during the 1990s and 2000s, as well as unwillingness to continue with the project after its dissatisfactory capabilities became apparent. With development in an advanced stage, parading mock-ups of the missile by way of deterrent instead of finalising it may have been preferential, at least until the decision was made to demonstrate a working example in the 2010s.

Nonetheless, there are numerous reports referring to alleged exports of the system to Iran, with the first such claims alleging up to 18 missiles were transferred as early as 2005.[40] Although these reports are highly suspicious given the very immature developmental stage of the system at that time, the fact that the Hwasong-10 was already offered for export was confirmed after the leaking of a report by a delegation from Myanmar which visited the DPRK in 2008, which included a reference to a Scud-F missile capable of attaining 3,000 kilometres in range, once again affirming the estimated capabilities

A Hwasong-10 missile is launched from its 12x12 TEL. Note the protective covers shielding the delicate wheels from damage by the exhaust flames: this measure was only added after earlier testing, prolonging preparation time by impeding easy access to the control panels. (KCBC)

of this missile.[41] [42] That this design was showcased in such manner at this time is remarkable however, as it had not yet been properly tested and would require various substantial modifications that may well have affected its performance before it could function properly. That at least the technology that formed the basis for the Hwasong-10 was exported to Iran was seemingly confirmed when it unveiled its own Khorramshahr IRBM after reports of a test in 2016. Although the missile seems to employ some of its own design solutions (notably lacking the grid fins that were a later addition to the North Korean design), the engine in particular conclusively gives away its origins. This suggests a peculiar progression of the Hwasong-10's development where the system was first deployed and exported in the early 2000s without any proper testing to affirm its capabilities, with such tests much later unveiling that significant work was still required on the design.

For all the new technologies the Hwasong-10 represented, it and older designs were similarly limited by an important aspect: they were all liquid-fuelled. Although liquid fuel is easier to produce and allows for a simpler rocket design, it delivers a lower thrust than solid fuel, is dangerous to work with and, perhaps most importantly, requires a lengthy fuelling process prior to launch during which the TEL and rocket may be spotted and attacked. As such, a switch to new solid-fuel designs, which could ultimately be used to create reliable and highly mobile long-ranged systems, was an obvious long-term goal for North Korean missile scientists to work towards. The first manifestation of such aspirations once again entailed the copying of a Soviet tactical ballistic missile, the 9K79 Tochka, which carries the North Korean designation of Hwasong-11 (alternately referred to as the KN-02 and 'Toksa' in the West) and was first seen during the parade for the 75th anniversary of the Korean People's Army in 2007. Its origins are, as with much of the DPRK's ballistic missile programme, subject to some debate, with many sources claiming either a transfer of technology or the actual systems themselves from Syria during the mid-1990s. However, direct Russian cooperation with development is also not implausible, considering other reverse engineering projects, such as the Kh-35 and S-300, that appear to have had Russian consent and possibly even assistance during the late 1990s and early 2000s. The story is further complicated by claims by the South Korean media that the Hwasong-11 was first successfully tested in May 2015 to a range of 120 kilometres, after a failed test in 2004, which would correspond with the upgraded 9M79-1 'Tochka-U' missile not in possession by Syria at the time.[43] However, these reports cannot be confirmed, and the external characteristics of the North Korean missile actually match with the original 9M79(M), which has a range of some 70 kilometres, a warhead weighing 482 kilogrammes and a CEP of roughly 150 metres.

Despite the fact that the missile itself appears to be externally identical to the 9M79, the chassis used for the Hwasong-11 could not differ more from the 9K79's amphibious BAZ-5921. Instead, it is based on a commercial Belarusian MAZ-630308 series 6x6 or 6x4 truck, once again indicating North Korea during this period experienced difficulties with producing heavy-duty TELs, and opted for an easier solution as a result. An added benefit of using this chassis, but also one that is to some degree inherent to the 9K79 system in general, is that the missile is completely covered in the chassis when it is not in launch position, making it difficult to differentiate the Hwasong-11 launcher from a regular commercial truck at a distance. Despite its short range, it was at the time of its introduction one of the more accurate long-ranged weapons systems in the North Korean army, and its high mobility and quick reaction time made it a potent weapon during wartime. Nonetheless, with the advent of the new 300mm MRL system and host of more advanced tactical missiles that followed, which feature a larger range, better accuracy and are capable of delivering more payload on multiple targets, the Hwasong-11 has lost much of its purpose in the KPA.

Although development of new solid-fuelled ballistic missiles would eventually eagerly be pushed ahead, the Hwasong-12 would in fact be another long-ranged liquid-fuelled design. This despite claims of a solid-fuelled missile being tested out to 220 and 240 kilometres in 2014 and 2015 which were supposedly tied to this system. Part of the confusion may stem from a spate of testing in 2014 and 2015 of short-ranged systems with similar ranges, some of which were of Hwasong-5s, but most were of the new 300mm MRL system which was tested out to an impressive range of up to 220 kilometres. This range alone would be enough for some to speculate about a different new missile, especially since details about

North Korean Hwasong-11 missiles paraded through Pyongyang on their TELs. Images of this missile actually being tested do not exist. (KCBC via Boaz Guttman)

the 300mm system had not yet become available. To make matters worse, North Korea's KCNA media outlet released doctored images purportedly of the 14 August test in 2014, showing what appeared to be a Hwasong-11 derived missile being launched to some 220 kilometres. Analysis of the images and this launch show that this was in fact an early test of the 300mm system however, which apparently was not ready to be shown to the public at this point. The true basis of its modern solid-fuelled ballistic missile programme was also in the making at this point, but would not, in fact, be found in the Hwasong missile family.

The actual Hwasong-12 (US DoD designation of KN-17) would only be unveiled during the parade for the 105th anniversary of Kim Il Sung's birthday in 2017, which debuted four separate ballistic missile systems that were hitherto unknown in a shock to international analysts. The unveiling of the Hwasong-12 was not entirely an unexpected development however, as the first indication that a missile in its class was under development actually came from a static engine test at North Korea's newly built engine test stand at the Sohae Satellite Launching Ground in September 2016. This was hailed as a new type of high-power engine, by the name of 'Paektusan', for a carrier rocket, with a document examined by Kim Jong Un claiming the design could generate 80 metric tonnes of thrust, over three times as much as the R-27's 4D10. Interestingly, analysis has shown the engine's design closely matches that of a series of engines from the NPO Energomash (Glushko) design bureau which included the Glushko RD-250, a Soviet dual-nozzle liquid rocket engine which was the basis of the RD-251 that powered the infamous R-36 'SS-18 Satan' ICBM.[44] Whether the North Korean engine like the RD-250 also uses the volatile NTO as opposed to the more stable IRFNA is doubtful, with images of tests of this engine often displaying the tell-tale red fumes from which IRFNA derives its name. As a result, an engine like the RD-219 that powered the second stage of the R-16 ICBM might be a more likely candidate. Whatever the case, the similarities are such that it can be stated confidently that the new North Korean engine is indeed heavily based on a product of this Russian design bureau. This implies either that North Korea obtained blueprints or a physical example after the fall of the Soviet Union, Russian/Ukrainian missile scientists were finding their way to the DPRK until quite recently, or that North Korean espionage

A photoshopped image of a purported upgraded Hwasong-11 being launched on 14 August 2014. In reality, a 300mm MRL system was tested. (KCBC)

is simply exceptionally successful in this area. The latter possibility should not be overlooked, as was witnessed by the conviction of two North Koreans accused of missile espionage in Ukraine in May 2012, including the stealing of confidential documents from the Yuzhnoye Design Office, which was responsible for designing the R-36 ICBM.[45] Another piece of the puzzle may be provided by reports of Iranian missile technicians visiting Pyongyang over 2013 to work on an '80-ton rocket booster', following commitments to strengthen defence, science and technology ties in late 2012.[46] The extent of the cooperation remains uncertain given that Iran did not seem to follow suit in introducing an Glushko-type engine for its ballistic missiles and satellite launch vehicles (SLVs). However, a defence capabilities exhibition held in Iran in January 2025 showcased a model of just such a two-chambered design at a display of its Simorgh SLV, finally lending firm credence to a link between the two countries' space and long-range missile programmes.

Interestingly, the September 2016 test only used a single nozzle, instead of the two used by the original Russian designs in order to mitigate the effects of combustion instability. Although the future

A static engine test is carried out at the Sohae Satellite Launching Ground. (KCBC)

The Glushko-type engine equipped with four vernier engines during the March 2017 static engine test. (KCBC)

would see the full dual-nozzle system also employed, another test in March 2017 which featured the same single nozzle variant of the engine accompanied by four vernier engines, the same type used by the R-27, would lay the basis for the Hwasong-12's propulsion. In keeping with the testing pattern of previous missiles, the Hwasong-12 itself was tested in a tight series of launches in April until the first success was publicised on 14 May, during which a missile was launched supposedly to a distance of 787 kilometres on a lofted trajectory, reaching a 2,111.5 kilometre apogee.[47] [48] This suggests that this single stage missile, which had a diameter of some 1.5 metres, flaring out to roughly 1.66 metres at the base, and a length of roughly 16 metres, is capable of reaching targets as far as up to 4,500 kilometres away. While its range made it, for a short period, the longest-ranged road-mobile ballistic missile in the North's arsenal, the design also actually introduces several other novelties that both increase and decrease its efficacy in their own ways. For one, although the missile is carried by the same modified MAZ-547W chassis used for the Hwasong-10, which was indeed oversized for this relatively small missile, the vehicle during testing actually functions as a transporter erector (TE) rather than a full-on TEL; prior to launch the missile is fixed to a prepared launch pad after which the TE drives away. This design choice is highly understandable given the difficulties North Korea had in procuring suitable TELs (which was a recurring limitation on military designs in all of its branches), and also because during test launches more than a few of these precious vehicles were believed to have been damaged extensively. This was reflected earlier during development of the Hwasong-10, whose TEL during its first successful test launch suddenly sported a thick protective covering over its wheels. Interestingly, this modification later also became the standard on the Hwasong-12's chassis alongside more thickly armoured instrument panels, and subsequent tests showcased the fact that these vehicles are in fact capable of being used as proper TELs during wartime. Without this capability the Hwasong-12 would be limited to a number of fixed launch sites across the country, and also suffer from an increased preparation time. Nevertheless, the final display of Hwasong-12s on their TELs during the 75th anniversary of the Workers' Party of Korea parade in 2020 showed them without the additional plating, the reason for which is unknown.

Another highly significant development is the introduction of a MaRV, which can be used to alter the warhead's flight trajectory in the mid or terminal flight sections. In so doing it thus deviates from its ballistic path, which aside from offering highly increased accuracy would make the warhead much harder to intercept.

Kim Jong Un salutes the crew of a MAZ-547W-inspired TEL after a successful Hwasong-12 test launch in September 2017. The damage to this vehicle as a result of previous test launches is apparent. Note the missing panel and the black markings on the now exposed rear wheel and the adjacent damaged panel. (KCBC)

Kim Jong Un watches as a Hwasong-12 missile is hoisted onto its TE(L). (KCBC)

Similar to the MaRV of the KN-10/KN-18, it likely uses GNSS guidance to attain a high degree of accuracy, although it is unsure whether this technology has been tested sufficiently for successful deployment yet. After the spate of testing in 2017 there were no publicised launch attempts of the Hwasong-12 until January 2022, and in general missile tests of groundbreaking North Korean designs appear to be aimed at showcasing the theoretical capabilities of the

While North Korea's copy of the MAZ-547W TE(L) for the Hwasong-10 and Hwasong-12 is in fact fully capable of launching missiles without the need of a prepared launch pad, damage sustained by several of these launchers during peacetime test launches likely means this capability will mostly be reserved for actual war. (NK Pro)

Some MAZ-547W-like chassis have undergone extensive modifications to improve their survivability against the sheer forces that occur during missile lift off and potential mishaps that can be expected to follow during test launches. (NK Pro)

A launch sequence of the Hwasong-12 missile. Note the potential for blast damage to the vehicle as seen in the third image, explaining why even with the additional shielding a fixed launch pad was used in a different test instead. (KCBC)

system more than actually testing its reliability. When the potency of a new design has been established through a successful test, resources are then often mostly diverted towards development of new systems rather than fine-tuning the original one. Still, the 2020s seemed to prove that North Korea found the Hwasong-12 design sufficiently capable and reliable to double down on its production, as was highlighted by a visit by Kim Jong Un in early 2023 to a missile production facility where at least 28 Hwasong-12 missiles were being assembled. Whether sufficient TELs for those missiles are available is questionable, and they have to share them with what appears to be an advanced offshoot of the Hwasong-12 tested in October 2022, attaining a range of 4,500 kilometres. This variant does away with the vernier engines to incorporate advances in engine gimballing, and seemingly has a smaller warhead. The problems encountered with the Hwasong-10 may well mean all modified MAZ-547W TELs will now be devoted to the Hwasong-12 family instead, effectively retiring the Hwasong-10 before it truly entered service.

By contrast, deployment of the Hwasong-12 immediately played a major role on the international stage as the North Korean press claimed on 8 August 2017 that a plan had been drafted for launching Hwasong-12 missiles to between 30 and 40 kilometres from Guam.[49] Apparently intended as a warning to the USA which maintains a massive military presence on Guam in the form of Andersen Air Force Base and Naval Base Guam, the threat came at the height of tensions between the two nations. While the order to execute the plan never came, during this time world observers collectively held their breath for what might well have elicited a nuclear war in a testament to the dangers North Korea's access to these new technologies brings.

A new type of liquid-fuelled IRBM launched in October 2022, overflying Japan. As there have been no publicised tests yet, little can be said about the missile other than that it evidently uses engine gimballing for steering, and seems to be based on the Hwasong-12. (KCBC)

The DPRK's apparent satisfaction with the success of the Hwasong-12 would come to expression in the 2020s with the introduction of a pair of advanced new weapons systems that were derived from it that sought to raise the bar for anti-ballistic missile defence systems. Although the existence of a programme for their development had already been alluded to during the 8th Congress of the Workers' Party of Korea (WPK) in early 2021, the first of two missile designs equipped with a hypersonic glide vehicle (HGV) was unveiled by its first flight test in September the same year. Confusingly, its name was reported as the Hwasong-8 – a designation which should have been given to a Hwasong-6 derivative decades ago. There remains as yet uncertainty about whether the North Koreans recycled the designation for this missile (which never entered service), or if the name stems from a misreporting. However, later displays of the same missile system at the 'Weaponry Exhibition-2023' in July 2023 referred to it more sensibly as the Hwasong-12Na (Hwasong-12B). While its conspicuously shaped payload on first appearance seems to be the most notable introduction to this Hwasong-12 derivative, the news commentary accompanying the test suggested that the first stage housed an equally important innovation. Despite seemingly utilising the same first stage as the Hwasong-12 base variant, the North Koreans claimed the addition of a so-called 'missile fuel ampoule', suggesting that missiles are filled with fuel and oxidiser at the factory and sealed hermetically to allow long-term storage of their sensitive propellants. If true, this would enable the missiles to respond far faster to a sudden launch order while utilising less specialised support equipment, given that its fuelling is then no longer required. The commentary further mentioned that former Marshal of the KPA Pak Jong Chon had 'noted the military significance of turning all missile fuel systems

Kim Jong Un inspects an underground missile facility where at least 28 partially assembled Hwasong-12s are stored in early 2023. (KCBC)

The Hwasong-12B at the Self-Defence-2021 exhibition, displayed alongside the Hwasong-12, Hwasong-15 and Hwasong-17, with the engine that powers the Hwasong-12 family displayed in front. (KCBC)

into ampoules', suggesting that this innovation will not remain confined to the Hwasong-12B. Both this modification and the substantial dimensions of the HGV will affect the missile's performance, and although the trajectory of its single known test flight is unknown foreign intelligence initially classified it as a short-range missile launch. It is uncertain whether the glide vehicle itself conducted any manoeuvres, and with the comparable Chinese DF-ZF HGV needing seven flight tests before entering operational service there is little doubt that the North Korean design will have to undergo much additional development before being deployed. Nevertheless, it would be unwise to dismiss the programme as mere fantasy, and the similarity to the Chinese DF-17 (which carries the DF-ZF) suggests the DPRK is attempting to go down a tried-and-proven development path. If the resemblance indeed translates to similar performance, the North Korean HGV can be expected to operate at speeds of up to Mach 10, re-entering the atmosphere at extreme speeds and then manoeuvring laterally to its target at high velocity. The hypersonic speeds, manoeuvrability and low-altitude approach to target means that such projectiles are typically considered impossible to intercept, making them valuable assets for disabling anti-ballistic missile defence systems or to deliver nuclear warheads. Nevertheless, North Korea's ability to evade or at least saturate such defences at the regional level can probably be considered more than sufficient, thus casting doubt on the additional utility of HGVs.

The second HGV-based Hwasong-12 offshoot, first displayed alongside the Hwasong-12B HGV in October 2021 at the Self-Defence-2021 exhibition, appears to embody a safer design approach. Though no name was ever reported for this type, it is possible that the (already recycled) designation Hwasong-8 was intended for it, with state media reports mixing up the two types. Alternatively, it may be that it is the Hwasong-12A. Images of flight tests showed this system installed on North Korea's 12x12 MAZ-547W-inspired TEL, a popular choice in the prototype stage, but soon a dedicated 12x12 TEL designed for both HGV types was unveiled. The cabin, instrument panelling and launch cabin in the mid-section of the TEL were redesigned, with the cabin now of a single joined type as opposed to the three separate ones of the earlier 12x12 variant. The depression in the roof of the cabin betrays that this vehicle was produced primarily for the Hwasong-12B HGV, as the shorter second type does not need it. Reportedly incorporating the same missile fuel ampoules as the Hwasong-12B, it utilises a shortened Hwasong-12 first stage to lift a dart-shaped nose cone equipped with four fins into a ballistic trajectory. Upon re-entering the atmosphere at around Mach 10, it makes a long lateral manoeuvre to approach its target at hypersonic speeds. Although this flight profile was supposedly tested twice in January 2022, the first time to a range of 700 kilometres with a lateral flight of 120 kilometres, and the second at a range of 1,000 kilometres, with a lateral flight of 240 kilometres, only the ballistic part of the trajectory was verified by foreign intelligence agencies (with Japanese tracking data suggesting a sharp turn was executed before an ocean splashdown). With the accurate simulation of HGVs typically demanding exorbitant processing power, it remains difficult to ascertain whether the North Korean approach is realistic. By hedging on two different designs, the odds of either succeeding have certainly improved. Nevertheless, the testing cadence has been characteristically unimpressive, making their operational deployment as of yet implausible. In fact, after their debuts, the programmes appeared to lie dormant until renewed testing of both HGVs from newly developed launch vehicles in 2024 and 2025.

The other liquid-fuelled HGV during one of its two known flight tests in January 2022. (KCBC)

Hwasong-12Bs during the 90th anniversary of the Korean People's Revolutionary Army in April 2022. (KCBC)

However shocking the rapid development of the Hwasong-12 and its novel technologies may have been, it was soon overshadowed by the dramatic entry of the DPRK's first road-mobile ICBM to the world stage. Breaking the satisfyingly sequential naming convention of the past years, the Hwasong-14 (US DoD designation of KN-20) made its debut both as an existing and as a flight-tested design to the international community on 3 July 2017. Nonetheless, it represents only a natural evolutionary step in North Korea's ballistic missile programme, and many of the technologies it employed were already exhibited on the Hwasong-12. Tested out to 933 kilometres on a lofted trajectory that gave it a 2,802 kilometre-high apogee, this missile combines the Hwasong-12's engine with a wider and longer body (some 1.7 by 19 metres), and adds a second stage to allow it to pass from IRBM into ICBM ranges, commonly defined as over 5,500 kilometres. A second test on 27 July 2017 reportedly investigated the full potential of the design, reaching an altitude of 3,724.9 kilometres and a range of 998 kilometres, affirming suspicions that the missile was capable of reaching far greater ranges than initially estimated. According to the KCNA statements on the test launch, one important modification was an increase of the number of engines on the second stage, presumably from two to three or four.[50] This alone could well account for the differences in performance. Although subject to some controversy, its maximum range is thought to be as high as 10,000 kilometres, sufficient to strike the entire western half of the USA.[51] [52] While this reason alone was enough to make headlines around the world and once again put North Korea's fledgling nuclear deterrent in the spotlight, the Hwasong-14 in fact represented only a transitional model for subsequent designs with even greater range and payload. One of the indicators that this was the case is its nose cone, which contrary to the Hwasong-12 appeared to consist of a so-called shroud rather than a hardened nose cone. Although a shroud, which has a much thinner hollow structure, may be used to carry a greater variety of payloads, including those that use decoys or even multiple warheads to increase the odds of defeating anti-ballistic missile defence systems, the example used on the Hwasong-14 would appear quite cramped for these purposes. Instead, it may have served as a testbed for one or more of these technologies so they could be applied to later, more powerful, ICBM designs.

Originally acquired as civilian vehicles optimised for construction purposes, the unmodified WS51200s were entirely unsuitable for use as a reusable TEL carrying liquid-fuelled missiles. (KCBC)

A Hwasong-14 missile is being erected by its TE(L) onto a fixed launch pad. (KCBC)

The TE(L) drives off to prevent it being damaged by the launch. (KCBC)

Another, perhaps more affirmative reason why the Hwasong-14 was unlikely to be a final product is a bit more elaborate, and is based on the transporter erector it employs. Purchased in November 2010 after two years of negotiations with the Wanshan Special Vehicle Company, six massive WS51200 16x12 trucks were first showcased during the parade for the 100th anniversary of Kim Il Sung's birthday in 2012, carrying the enormous Hwasong-13 missile. Barely trumped in extravagance by the missiles they transported, at a length of over 20 metres and an unprecedented 16 massive wheels, these vehicles have been used to transport almost all ICBM designs shown by the DPRK since. For this purpose they receive extensive modifications each time a new design requires their use, and there does not appear to be a common consensus as to which missile system is ultimately to deserve their permanent service. Since at the time the Hwasong-14 was first tested five of the WS51200s had been converted for another canister-based missile design showcased in the parade for the 105th anniversary of Kim Il Sung's birthday in 2017, only one was actually available for the tests, and it therefore seemed unlikely the Hwasong-14 would ever be operationally deployed on this platform. Tellingly, during the parade for the 70th anniversary of the founding of the Korean People's Army in 2018 four Hwasong-14s were displayed on massive flatbed trucks instead, without any mechanism for erecting them. The WS51200s were also displayed, albeit in hardly recognisable form, and as part of a system which yet surpassed any expectation about North Korea's road-mobile ICBM programme.

The Hwasong-14 might represent a transitional model for subsequent designs, having already been superseded by more capable designs shortly after its inception. Nonetheless, five missiles were present during the February 2018 parade in a demonstration of its fledgling long-ranged deterrent. (KCBC)

Much preceding these developments however, the originally intended recipient of the WS51200 platform, the Hwasong-13 (US DoD designation KN-08), was likely conceived of in the late 2000s. Aiming to use a complicated engine and an ambitious design in order to become the first North Korean ICBM, it drew widespread foreign attention years prior to the successes gained using the new Glushko-type engine as a basis. Given the remarkable design criteria, North Korean inexperience with building ICBMs and inconsistencies between examples paraded on the 100th anniversary of Kim Il Sung's birthday in 2012, it is not surprising that some analysts suspected the missiles were part of a misinformation campaign. Footage of Kim Jong Il inspecting prototypes of this intricate three-staged design and even an early example mounted on one of North Korea's, obviously outmatched, MAZ-547W-inspired TELs indicates that the programme was genuine however. Furthermore, it apparently predated the delivery of the WS51200 TE(L)s, and was in the pipelines far before any of the DPRK's modern missile systems had even been tested. Evidently, the programme ran into problems that severely set back development of the Hwasong-13, the reasons for which are likely to be entirely analogous to those that plagued the Hwasong-10 programme. Indeed, the engine that was to power the Hwasong-13 consisted of two of the Hwasong-10's 4D10s closely fitted together in what must have been an incredibly painstaking process of redesign, given that the original 4D10 was already uniquely complex due to its initial Soviet requirements as an SLBM engine. Although this engine would have provided the thrust required to get a large missile such as the Hwasong-13, which is close to two metres in diameter and some 18 metres long, off the ground, the fact that even the 'regular' 4D10 engine as used on the Hwasong-10 took until 2016 to work to any acceptable degree showed the far-reaching technological difficulties its implementation would entail. The first publicised static engine test came in April 2016, at which point development of missiles using the Glushko-derived engine was proceeding at a much faster pace.[53] In the meantime, the surprising three-staged design was replaced by a more sensible, yet theoretically shorter-ranged, two-staged design first showcased in the parade for the 70th anniversary of the founding of the Workers' Party of Korea in 2015.[54] This second missile design (US DoD designation KN-14), which retains the Hwasong-13 designation, uses the same first stage engine and is of the same diameter as its predecessor. However, it is some two metres shorter and forgoes the intricately shaped nose cone for a much simpler blunt one atop its second stage. In general, the substantial redesign appears to have been aimed at simplifying the Hwasong-13 design as much as possible in an attempt to salvage the programme, albeit in the end apparently to no avail. While it is uncertain whether the Hwasong-13 has been definitively cancelled, it appears likely that it and quite possibly the entire 4D10-based missile line are now scrapped in favour of the newcomers using the Glushko-derived engines. The advantage of this simpler design is directly evident in the stunningly fast progress of the last few years, and although the dual 4D10 engine would have provided slightly more thrust than the single-chamber Glushko-type engine, far more ambitious future designs may lay in the pipeline using the latter than would have been possible with only the 4D10. Nevertheless, both Hwasong-13 designs will likely have been instrumental in the DPRK's pursuit of an operational ICBM, and their estimated ranges of over 11,500 kilometres for the first variant and 10,000 kilometres for the second showed clearly for the first time the direction in which its ambitions were headed.[55]

The distinctly shaped nose cone and body of the original three-staged design of the Hwasong-13, with a mock-up of its nuclear warhead seen close behind. (KCBC)

Interestingly, the same facility also housed numerous bodies of the redesigned two-staged Hwasong-13, presumably being prepared for a parade. (KCBC)

Two two-staged Hwasong-13s paraded on their WS51200 TE(L)s during the 70th anniversary of the founding of the Workers' Party of Korea parade in 2015. (KCBC)

These ambitions unexpectedly came to a culmination in the fall of 2017. So shortly after the Hwasong-14 tests of July, many expected the launch of 29 November to be of the same type, perhaps modified to squeeze the optimal performance out of the design. Instead, they were treated to one of the largest road-mobile ICBMs ever built. At a length of over 24 metres and a diameter of well over two metres, this two-staged behemoth outsizes other contemporary road-mobile ICBMs such as the Russian RS-24 Yars or Chinese DF-41. Its initial test launch appears to have been a success, flying to an altitude of 4,475 kilometres over a distance of 950 kilometres in 53 minutes – statistics that in a subsequent test in February 2023 were improved to a maximum altitude of 5,768.5 kilometres and a distance of 989 kilometres in nearly 67 minutes. Estimates about what capabilities this might translate to on a more conventional trajectory vary, but there is little debate that the Hwasong-15 (US DoD designation of KN-22) would be capable of targeting the entire US mainland with a payload of 1,000 kilogrammes. The key to this substantial increase in capabilities over the Hwasong-14 is its engine, which consists of a double-nozzled (as opposed to the one chamber engines of the Hwasong-12 and Hwasong-14) Glushko-type engine clone that is gimballed to provide steering. This is the same 'Paektusan' engine that was tested in September 2016 supposedly for use on an SLV, now providing the thrust required to lift the missile's two stages into the skies. The composition of the second stage, which has the same diameter as the first, is largely unknown, likely using two smaller indigenously developed engines for its propulsion. As with many of the DPRK's most recent ballistic missile designs, it is expected to use a MaRV to precisely lead its warhead to its target. However, its large nose cone and heavy throw weight also pave the way for another coveted technology associated with ballistic missile-delivered WMDs: Multiple Independently-targetable Re-entry Vehicles (MIRVs). This means a single missile may be capable of carrying multiple warheads which are then guided towards different targets, thus vastly increasing the amount of damage inflicted.[56] That such technology is indeed where North Korean ambitions lie was confirmed during the 8th Congress of the WPK in January 2021, where it was noted that 'research into perfecting the guidance technology for multi-warhead rocket at the final stage' was being conducted.[57] Another, more simple option however is to add a number of decoys to the missile's payload, serving to complicate efforts to intercept the warhead on its descent. Such techniques could greatly enhance the success rate of an ICBM's warheads at comparatively little cost, and are likely to be in advanced stages of development already. One other possible new design element currently present is quite significant, and might for the first time have properly been tested on the Hwasong-15. Whereas many liquid-fuelled ballistic missiles require fuelling on site after erection, it appears the North Koreans may have managed to enable it to be fuelled even while the vehicle is still in its shelter, thus minimising the amount of time it is exposed to foreign intelligence from the air. Nevertheless, like the Hwasong-14 it cannot be used without causing some degree of damage to its launcher, and the only solution to sparing it is using pre-prepared hardened launch pads (though blast deflectors were installed to mitigate this problem to a degree). A February 2023 test of the Hwasong-15 supposedly conducted to prove the response time of the DPRK's nuclear forces after a surprise order to launch did see the missile launched directly from its TEL however. The claims of unpreparedness of the 'First Red Flag' Hero Company involved in the firing should be taken with a grain of salt however, as the launch location at the DPRK's international airport was presumably not its intended operational area. Furthermore, the same launcher was likely used for a more experimental launch of a modified Hwasong-15 in November 2022, which reportedly tested the reliability of a warhead with a special function that paralyses the enemy's operational command system – presumably a nuclear weapon designed to employ the high-altitude electromagnetic pulse (HEMP) effect (more on which in the section on WMDs).[58] This launch was also notable because the missile no longer sported the slightly flaring skirts around the engine that had been the norm for North Korean ICBMs up until that point, which are thought to have increased stability of the missile at a slight performance cost. The fact that this inefficiency was now solved is another testament to the fact that the Hwasong-15 and other missiles continue to benefit from incremental improvements.

To carry these massive road-mobile ICBMs, the WS51200s imported from China had to be completely overhauled. All of the hydraulics, instrument panels and the driver's cabin have been replaced and perhaps most impressively, an entire new axle was added between the third and the fourth from the rear. The resulting 18x12 TE(L) was at the time of its introduction quite likely the largest missile carrier in the world, although it may well have struggled to properly handle the weight of its burden given that it presumably still uses the original 685 horsepower engine. Four of these massive vehicles and their missiles were displayed during the parade for the 70th anniversary of the founding of the Korean People's Army in 2018; the other two WS51200s available were likely already in the process of conversion to yet another new project. The careful dance that North Korea is performing with these vehicles to support its ICBM development programme while making it appear as though large numbers of road-mobile ICBMs with associated launch vehicles are already entering service is notable, and should rightly elicit some scepticism. With the WS51200s now displayed between only short intervals with six different ICBM designs (for which the vehicles were completely overhauled five times), it may be safely assumed that only the vehicle responsible for operationally testing each design is actually outfitted with the required equipment. To complete the ruse, the North Koreans have now multiple times displayed five of the six vehicles in an overhauled state, while keeping one in its original configuration to launch a missile of the previous design in an apparent attempt to convince the outside world of its operational status. Whether the WS51200s were ever intended to become part of North Korea's operational nuclear deterrent is unknown, and it could well be that aside from enabling the launch of perhaps one ICBM at any time the other vehicles served for development and propaganda purposes only. For a true road-mobile deterrent, these complex and imposing vehicles needed to enter indigenous production, for which North Korea provided little evidence beyond showcasing the indigenous manufacture of its tyres. With the WS51200s soon repurposed yet again, as of 2024 there is no indication that dedicated TELs for the Hwasong-15 remain. Instead, the DPRK soon set its aims even higher to finally truly unshackle its road-mobile ICBM force.

Hwasong-15s paraded through Pyongyang on their TELs during the 70th anniversary of the founding of the KPA parade on 8 February 2018. (KCBC)

The only known launch of a modified Hwasong-15, supposedly to test a warhead that exploits the HEMP effect. Note the lack of a flared base. (KCBC)

Note how new wheel caps have been fitted to the Hwasong-15's TE, possibly to mask the fact that the WS51200 is the basis for this behemoth. (KCBC)

A Hwasong-15 missile while being set up on its launching pad. (KCBC)

Another image of the Hwasong-15 under preparation for its first test flight. The next, in February 2023, would be its last. (KCBC)

In most countries that have undertaken the herculean efforts required to establish a functional nuclear deterrent, the prospect of operationally deploying a road-mobile ICBM as large as the Hwasong-15 would have been daunting, and perhaps even undesirable for reasons of practicality. Though substantially larger ICBMs can and have been built, their size typically precludes this method of deployment, and they are more sensibly found in dedicated launch silos. The 2020s were about to provide military analysts that adhere to this line of thought some perspective on what the DPRK does and does not consider sensible however. As the dust settled from the four oversized Hwasong-15 TELs with their almost comically large payloads that passed the stands during the 75th anniversary of the Workers' Party of Korea parade in 2020, the headlights of a monstrosity that was larger still shone blindingly in the distance. At a total length of some 30 metres, or about three double-decker buses, and a width of about 4 metres (not to mention a height almost twice that), this system can only be called truly road-mobile for those roads that have been checked for obstacles and structural integrity beforehand. Needless to say, the advent of the Hwasong-17 was an unexpected development to most observers. Nevertheless, new developments in the field of ICBMs were to some degree anticipated, with an unclassified Russian intelligence briefing earlier that year already suggesting that North Korea was undertaking the sensible step of introducing two of the powerful Glushko-type engines that power the Hwasong-15 to a single missile. That this missile would receive its own indigenously produced 11-axle 22x16 TEL instead of a fixed launch silo only became apparent when it was unveiled to the world, definitively proving the DPRK was capable of moving beyond the handful of Chinese launch vehicles acquired abroad. It would take until 24 March 2022 before the Hwasong-17 was actually tested however, and even then the success of its debut launch was somewhat controversial. Though a missile did attain an altitude of 6,248.5 kilometres and a horizontal displacement of 1,090 kilometres over the course of some 67.5 minutes, South Korean intelligence alleges that the system in question was in fact a Hwasong-15, with its launch meant to conceal an embarrassing failure of the Hwasong-17 that occurred on 16 March.[59] Whether this was indeed the case or not remains unclear, and North Korea would demonstrate the Hwasong-17 again in November the same year, as well as in March the next. Although this should dispel most doubts about the operational status of this ICBM, the fact that significant changes are still being introduced to its design was attested by each of its launches. Curiously, between the first and the second test, the size ratios of the first and second stages were significantly altered, perhaps suggesting that the second stage propulsion had been changed. Though the ratios would remain the same for the second and third tests, the latter for the first time showed the Hwasong-17 without the flared base that other North Korean IRBMs and ICBMs had sported, and that was now apparently no longer a requirement for ensuring the missile's stability.

With the Hwasong-15 already theoretically capable of striking the entirety of the mainland US, and the theoretical range increase only bringing into range parts of South America and Southern Africa, the additional utility of the Hwasong-17 is perhaps questionable. Although the most plausible explanation is that the intended use of the Hwasong-17 is to deliver supersized (and MIRV) warheads, the fact remains that the Hwasong-15 should have been able to deliver substantial payloads already. Moreover, the size increase to a diameter of approximately 2.8 metres and a length of some 26 metres brings with it substantial difficulties, not least of which the exorbitant costs of both missile and launcher. Furthermore, its dimensions will complicate its operations and thereby lengthen its crucially important response time, both because of the difficulty in relocating it and the substantial amount of fuel and oxidiser that need to be loaded prior to launch. To mitigate these detrimental effects, North Korea appears to be able to transport these missiles at least some distance while refuelled, erecting them at the launch site without needing a small army of fuelling and support vehicles. Furthermore, a massive blast deflecting shield built into the launcher seems to negate the need for it to move out of dodge before firing. Though the sudden appearance of the largest road-mobile ICBM in history might be of value in and of itself to the DPRK's deterrent, it is possible that another reason exists for its oversized proportions. With North Korea itself declaring a goal of being able to strike with 'pinpoint' accuracy any target within 15,000 kilometres during the 8th Congress of the WPK in 2021, it may be that the Hwasong-17 is intended to be used in such a manner that the payload effectively reaches orbit before propelling itself down to its target. Known as a Fractional Orbital Bombardment System, this method of operation would allow the DPRK to launch nuclear armament over the South Pole and thus approach the US from its southern border, in the process evading elements of the Ground-Based Midcourse Defence (GMD) designed to intercept ICBM warheads.

Whatever the exact technologies intended to be fitted under the Hwasong-17's large shroud, its advent marks the point where

MGB personnel process the launch order from the Hwasong-17s control vehicle during its first test in March 2022. (KCBC)

A Hwasong-17 in flight during its first test in March 2022, clearly displaying the two clustered RD-250-derived engines. (KCBC)

Kim Jong Un and his daughter Kim Ju Ae inspect a Hwasong-17 prior to its second publicised flight in November 2022. (KCBC)

Kim Jong Un guides a Russian delegation through a showroom at the Weaponry Exhibition-2023. In front, the Saetbyol-4 and Saetbyol-9 U(C)AVs. In the back, a Hwasong-17 in a new livery (still with the flared base) as well as a Hwasong-18. (KCBC)

Hwasong-17s during the 75th anniversary of the foundation of the Korean People's Army in February 2023. The procession of colossi seemed unending. (KCBC)

North Korea's long-range strategic deterrent has become all but impossible to deny. Although the lengthy preparation (which was well over 9 hours for the 'surprise' Hwasong-15 launch in February 2023 if North Korean news commentary is to be believed), scarce testing and the various layers of ballistic missile defences that these systems are likely to face might mean that not all can be deployed successfully, the 12 Hwasong-17s mustered for the 75th anniversary of the foundation of the Korean People's Army in February 2023 alone should cast serious doubt on successful premature destruction in the event of war. Images taken during visits by Kim Jong Un to a TEL production facility in 2023 and 2024 suggested another eight TELs were assembled since then, implying a production capacity of approximately one every two months, notwithstanding manufacture of the missiles themselves.[60]

Alongside the series of successes in the development of long-ranged road-mobile ballistic missiles, North Korea was shockingly revealed to have been simultaneously working on the debut of another leg of its nuclear triad in late 2014. In a programme based out of its eastern port of Sinpho, close to the massive Mayang Do submarine base, the DPRK's first ballistic missile submarines (or SSBs; sub-surface ballistic) and associated SLBM systems were produced and extensively tested, at least to North Korean standards. For this purpose, an extensive test site was erected ashore which would host a range of ejection tests and launches over the years, with a test barge patterned after the Soviet PSD-series providing data on actual submerged launches. A spate of land-based tests in late 2014 were followed by sea-based ones in early 2015, and on 9 May 2015 North Korea first publicised images of an SLBM test supposedly conducted from an SSB. Although analysis showed it was actually launched from the test barge instead, the images gave an interesting first look at the direction in which the DPRK's ambitions were heading. Evidently liquid-fuelled, the missile had a diameter of about 1.25 metres and a length of 8.5 metres, and appeared to use a simple rocket engine, perhaps derivative of its early Hwasong programme. Inscribed on the missile was the designation Pukguksong-1 (US DoD designation KN-11), meaning Polaris/North Star-1 in Korean: a clear jab at the USA's own initial SLBM programme of the 1950s which spawned the first ever operational SLBM under the designation of UGM-27 Polaris. Intriguingly, the engine of the Hwasong-10, whose design was actually once created for use on an SLBM, was not used, possibly due to the difficulties the DPRK had faced getting it to work properly even ashore. However, the key technology which enables most SLBM launches was perhaps the more important technology tested: a gas generator was employed to allow the missile to do a cold launch, whereby it is first ejected through the water into the air before the main engine is ignited. This process can be quite rough, and is therefore usually not compatible with liquid-fuelled missiles, which may be attested by one or two failed tests conducted in late 2015, of which it is unclear whether they resulted in damage to the submarine or barge.

Solid-Fuelled Ballistic Missiles

A test of a solid-fuelled rocket engine on 23 March 2016 was therefore highly foreboding of new developments to come.[61] And indeed, exactly one month later another SLBM test was conducted, this time of a missile that despite having the same dimensions and external characteristics of the Pukguksong-1, was in fact solid-fuelled and carried the almost identical designation of Pukguksong (yet lacking a numerator).[62] What is more, at this point it became apparent that the Pukguksong was in fact a two-staged design, and

A Pukguksong/Polaris SLBM being tested, possibly from a submerged barge. Note that the engine is only ignited in the third frame, after expulsion from the launch tube and the ocean. (KCBC)

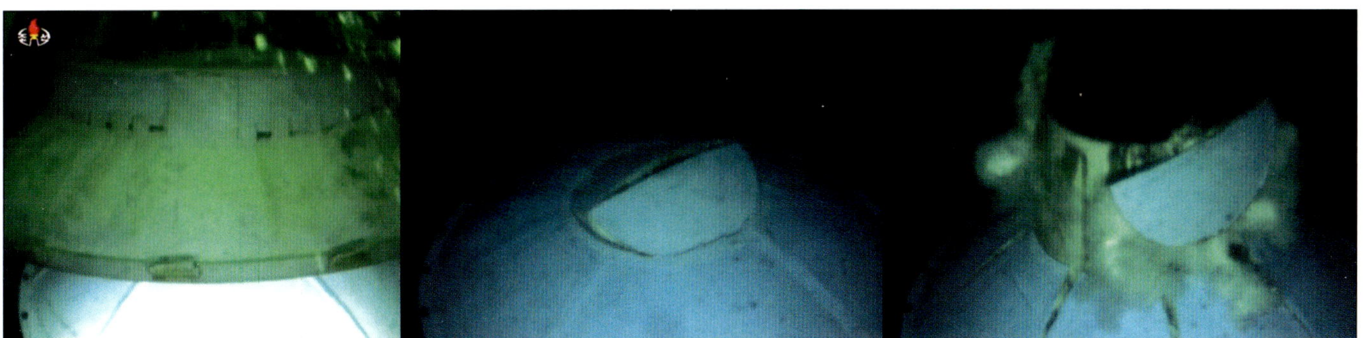

A Pukguksong/Polaris SLBM being expelled from its submerged launch tube. (KCBC)

at the time the first expressly military-tested missile to have more than one stage at that. Although the test of April only saw a missile launched to some 30 kilometres in distance, a subsequent launch on 24 August lobbed the Pukguksong's payload to a much more impressive range of 500 kilometres. Even still, it was believed to have used a lofted trajectory which gave it an apogee of up to 550 kilometres, resulting in a maximum range on a normal trajectory of as much as 1,250 kilometres.[63] This is sufficient to target the entirety of Korea and Japan with a warhead of over 500 kilogrammes, providing the DPRK with a nuclear deterrent that is very difficult to detect or shoot down. Although just a single SSB with a single launch tube was available as a launch platform, this has not stopped the DPRK from parading a multitude of Pukguksongs on flatbed trucks. Interestingly, high resolution photos of these missiles showed yet another new technology premiered on this ambitious design which has the potential to substantially increase the efficiency of North Korean solid-fuelled ballistic missiles. An August 2017 visit to the Chemical Material Institute of the Academy of Defence Sciences by Kim Jong Un confirmed that wound-filament casings were being produced. These consist of tightly woven carbon fibres which can produce an incredibly strong yet lightweight structure, ideal for the type of pressures solid-fuel tanks and engines need to endure while keeping the missile's inert mass as low as possible. This not only increases the performance of existing solid-fuelled designs, it also paves the way for much larger classes of missiles which would not be able to function satisfactorily using regular casings. Despite introducing a multitude of highly significant new technologies, there is no indication that the Pukguksong(-1) remains in use, with other improved designs seemingly having succeeded the missile in recent years, including on the one SSB capable of launching it.

A solid-fuelled MRBM that could be ready to strike much of the region at a moment's notice would certainly have seemed desirable to the MGB not only at sea but also on land. It is therefore not surprising that the Pukguksong-2, which was first tested successfully

A Pukguksong SLBM paraded through the streets of Pyongyang. Note that the gas ejector is still attached to the missile here, and that eight grid fins similar to the ones also seen on the Hwasong-10 and other solid-fuelled missile designs have been added. (NK Pro)

on 11 February 2017 took precisely this form.[64] What is surprising however, is that despite expectations the Pukguksong-2 turned out not to be merely a land-based variant of the Pukguksong, but in fact constitutes a larger design of some 1.5 metres in diameter and 9.5 metres in length. Nevertheless, its two tests, the second of which occurred on 21 May 2017, both utilised comparable trajectories with an apogee of some 560 kilometres and a range of 500 kilometres, almost identical to the August 2016 Pukguksong launch. Although a likely increase in payload size to the 1,000 kilogramme range or larger (given the size of the redesigned nose cone) is partially to blame, it is possible we have yet to see the full potential of this system. Nevertheless, even without increases in range the Pukguksong-2 would be able to target both Korea and much of Japan from anywhere in the DPRK, further securing its regional nuclear deterrent.

Another auspicious new development that was pioneered on the Pukguksong-2 was its heavy-duty tracked TEL, an offshoot of the new Songun tank production line. Produced at the Kusong tank plant, and possibly responsible for a snag in production of the tanks also built there, the TEL measures some nine metres in length and adds an armoured cabin, instrument panels and two road wheels to the ordinary Songun tank chassis. Due to this commonality it is easier to produce than the wheeled TELs previously used for most of the mobile ballistic missiles, without sacrificing off-road capabilities. The parade for the 105th anniversary of Kim Il Sung's birthday in April 2017 already featured seven of these impressive vehicles, which are curiously reminiscent of the TEL used for the Soviet RT-20P ICBM, and their launch systems, while Kim Jong Un decreed that following the May 2017 test mass production of the Pukguksong-2 should rapidly commence.[65] Although a lack of further testing in the years since has cast some doubt on this statement, the Pukguksong-2 remains one of the more potent missile designs that has entered service with the MGB, combining a large payload with capable medium-ranged flight characteristics and the advantages in reliability and preparation time that solid-fuelled ballistic missiles bring. Furthermore, it should be easier to produce in numbers than many previous designs in the same class, and very difficult to track due to its off-road capabilities. Despite these advantageous characteristics, the Pukguksong-2 has neither been tested nor displayed since the start of the new decade, and it appears focus has shifted towards production of its more modern successors.

The SLBM programme continued in parallel with development of the Pukguksong-2 in search of a missile suited for the next generation SSB under construction at the Sinpho shipyard. Scarce imagery from a concert in celebration of the first successful Hwasong-14 launch in July 2017 as well as a poster seen during Kim Jong Un's visit to the Chemical Material Institute of the Academy of Defence Sciences detailed some of the specifications of the programme. The former revealed that at least two ejection tests had been completed at the Sinpho land-based test stand as well as a newly erected test stand on a tank test track near the Kusong tank plant, where the Pukguksong-2 was also first launched. The two-staged design subtly showcased on the poster once again represented a substantial size increase over the Pukguksong, at a diameter of just shy of two metres and a length of over 12 metres. This means that the Pukguksong-3 would require new testing barges to conduct submerged tests from, and indeed, such a new testing barge has been spotted at Nampho since April 2017 and was finished in November that year. The missile also clearly outgrew the Gorae-class as a testing platform, and the next generation SSB would likely require a raised platform or a similar construction to the Gorae-class whereby the missile launch

The Pukguksong-2 tracked TEL prior to its first test. Note the protective cover on the launch tube that will be blown off before erecting. (KCBC)

A Pukguksong-2 being tested on 11 February 2017. The blast shown is created by the gas generator expelling the missile from its launch tube; ignition of the main engine occurs a second or so later. (KCBC)

tube is fitted in the conning tower, or missiles of this size will not fit. The pay-off for the size increases could be great however, potentially providing the DPRK with a much more capable platform for striking targets such as the US military bases on Guam and beyond. The sole test launch of the Pukguksong-3 in October 2019 showed a substantially reworked design, which aside from sporting an all-black two stage body swapped the pointed or triconic nose cone for a large payload shroud. With a reported lofted trajectory ranging out to 450 kilometres and an apogee of 910 kilometres, the missile is believed to have been capable of attaining a range of at least 1,900 kilometres when fired on a regular trajectory. With the test believed to have been conducted from a submerged barge off the coast of Wonsan for this occasion, it is possible that renewed testing is now awaiting the completion of its new launch platform(s). With missile designs seemingly being iterated upon at a much higher pace than work is progressing on its SSBs, it is possible that the Pukguksong-3 will be replaced by a more advanced derivative before it has a chance to be operationally deployed.

The 2020s would see a rapid succession of new additions to the Pukguksong missile family marked by a notable absence of any publicised tests. The parades of 2020, 2021 and 2022 would introduce the Pukguksong-4S, Pukguksong-5S and another unnamed Pukguksong variant, each time presented on the same progressively more outsized truck-towed trailers. All three share the same diameter of a little over two metres and carbon fibre wound-filament construction, but shifting stage lengths and

An image of a possible Pukguksong-3 SLBM being loaded by cranes prior to a land-based (ejection) test at the test stand near Sinpho. Another similar test was performed at a test stand near the Kusong tank test track. (KCBC)

What is believed to be a significantly reworked Pukguksong-3 is launched from a submerged barge in October 2019. (KCBC)

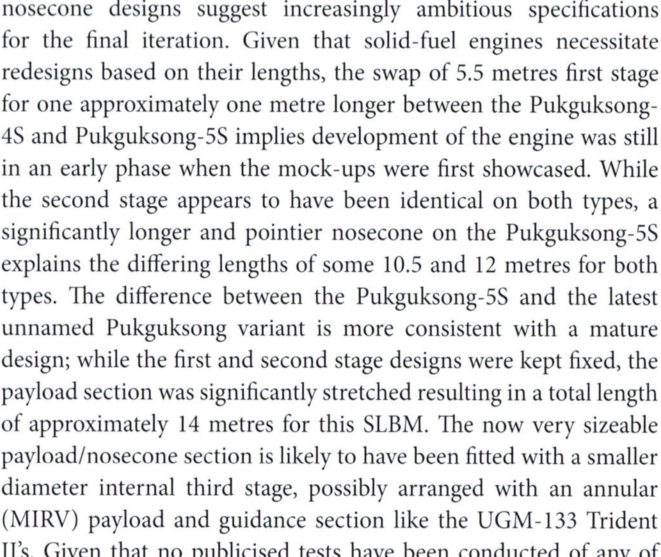

nosecone designs suggest increasingly ambitious specifications for the final iteration. Given that solid-fuel engines necessitate redesigns based on their lengths, the swap of 5.5 metres first stage for one approximately one metre longer between the Pukguksong-4S and Pukguksong-5S implies development of the engine was still in an early phase when the mock-ups were first showcased. While the second stage appears to have been identical on both types, a significantly longer and pointier nosecone on the Pukguksong-5S explains the differing lengths of some 10.5 and 12 metres for both types. The difference between the Pukguksong-5S and the latest unnamed Pukguksong variant is more consistent with a mature design; while the first and second stage designs were kept fixed, the payload section was significantly stretched resulting in a total length of approximately 14 metres for this SLBM. The now very sizeable payload/nosecone section is likely to have been fitted with a smaller diameter internal third stage, possibly arranged with an annular (MIRV) payload and guidance section like the UGM-133 Trident II's. Given that no publicised tests have been conducted of any of the three systems, but a largely identical SLBM model to the latest design was again showcased at the 'Military Hardware Exhibition Defence Development-2025', it may be assumed this design is to be the definitive iteration deployed on North Korea's newest SSBN. Its dimensions are broadly consistent with (or slightly in excess of) three-staged SLBMs deployed by major powers, and may be assumed to be of intercontinental range. Moreover, they are a good match for the dimensions of the missile tubes on the SSBN, which are thought to be no longer than 16 metres. Although significant testing is required to realistically establish this SLBM as a long-ranged nuclear deterrent, the rough correspondence of its first and second stage dimensions with those of the second and third stages of the Hwasong-19 ICBM (as well as the carbon fibre wound-filament construction) imply a possible overlap in development. However, where the pace of North Korean solid-fuelled missile development has at times defied all reasonable expectations, actual integration tests with its submarines have not always gone as smoothly, and will pose a significant challenge.

A Pukguksong-5S (left) alongside Pukguksong-1 and Hwasong-11S SLBMs. (KCBC)

Pukguksong-4S SLBMs towed during the 75th anniversary of the Workers' Party of Korea parade in 2020. (KCBC)

An unnamed Pukguksong variant during the 90th anniversary of the founding of the Korean People's Revolutionary Army in 2022, presumed to be the Pukguksong-6S. (KCBC)

Just prior to the hiatus in missile tests brought on by the focus on diplomacy in 2018, another solid-fuelled system that would later prove to have far-reaching potential was showcased during the parade for the 70th anniversary of the founding of the Korean People's Army. Six new Taebaeksan TELs each carrying two hitherto unseen missiles drove past the parade grounds, in an ominous early incarnation of what would eventually materialise as a very tangible new missile system. Although a first test was initially barred by diplomacy, the external characteristics of these missiles left little doubt about their intended role and aspired capabilities. Almost identical in shape, size and even the general layout of the launch vehicle, they closely resemble the infamous Russian 9K720 Iskander SRBM. Two tests in May 2019 and another two in late July and early August, which saw eight of the new missiles being launched on trajectories very similar to that of the 9K720 Iskander-M's 9M723K1 missile, affirmed that the system is indeed capable of matching at least some of the auspicious characteristics its external appearance suggested. Despite the far-going similarities to the Russian 9K720 Iskander however, details in the system's construction differ in many aspects, and the cable raceway, usually indicative of which part of a missile contains propellant, extends far past where it ends in both directions on a regular Iskander missile. More importantly, although the missile's aspect ratios match the Iskander's well enough, it appears it is almost 20 percent larger at a length of some 8.6 metres and a diameter of 1.1 metres. This difference is sufficient to discredit any substantial link with its Russian inspiration beyond using shared technologies, and actually suggests that the new missile uses an engine potentially derived from the one used by the Pukguksong-1.[66] Its external similarity to the Iskander then serves mainly to confuse foreign observers, and perhaps simply to give the impression that the DPRK is capable of matching any ballistic missile system fielded by other nations across the globe. It bears noting that the system is considered in North Korea to be part of the Hwasong-11 missile family (US DoD designation KN-23), bearing the designation Hwasong-11Ka (Hwasong-11A, according to the North Korean alphabet), despite the missile having no direct relation to the Tochka-derived Hwasong-11. Still, its layout and operation are similar, and some of the technologies incorporated in its design originated from the Hwasong-11 much as design elements of the 9K79 Tochka were also found in the 9K714 Oka which in turn evolved into the 9K720 Iskander. In this sense, the Hwasong-11Ka is technologically more similar to the Tochka than it is to the Iskander. It bears further noting that the carbon fibre wound-filament casing of the Pukguksong series was foregone for this missile, evidently due to lower weight requirements and to facilitate easier production. This, as well as the hot launch mode, might conceivably explain the odd naming scheme that has this missile part of the Hwasong series as opposed to the Pukguksong series.

In the 2020s, test and training launches of this missile system and its derivatives would begin occurring at a very high frequency, from a multitude of different platforms. With the number of distinct mobile launchers of this missile family displayed at one time or another numbering in the hundreds, it now plausibly constitutes the mainstay of the North Korean short-ranged ballistic missile arsenal. The diversity of platforms, variants and mission profiles showcased evidently underlines the fact that the DPRK has elected to make this missile family the central component of its short-ranged deterrent, transplanting (though not outright replacing) the earlier Scud and Tochka-derived missiles in this role. In its original configuration, the Hwasong-11A can utilise either an 8x8 wheeled platform or a tracked chassis derived from the Songun tank chassis but with eight road wheels. Repeated tests and displays during parades would unveil a range of slightly different cabs and chassis, with the original truck-based Taebaeksan platforms soon making way for MAZ-543-style heavy launchers. Although the introduction of these heavy TELs is an indicator that the DPRK is making substantial progress in resolving its issues with the production of military-grade heavy vehicles, the fact that these vehicles have continued to evolve over time simultaneously highlights that true mass production has not commenced, with North Korea seemingly forever stuck in the low-rate initial production phase with many such projects.

It is believed the Hwasong-11A is compatible with more than one size of warhead, with missile tests at times conducted at shorter ranges of around 250 and 450 kilometres, for which a warhead of upwards of 1,500 kilogrammes may be employed, and at times much greater ones of as much as 800 kilometres, which could have utilised a warhead of 500 kilogrammes or less. All of its launches have shared the common characteristic of using a depressed trajectory however, with missiles attaining a maximum altitude of between 30 and 60 kilometres at most.[67] Although this suggests a maximum range well into MRBM territory (1,000 kilometres or higher), it is likely the system is intended for use with depressed trajectories only, ideal for evading anti-ballistic missile defences such as Aegis, Patriot and THAAD, which have difficulty in engaging targets at this height. To further aid it in this capacity, the missile system incorporates advanced capabilities such as manoeuvrability during its entire flight path, and the ability to perform a pull-up manoeuvre in mid flight, thus technically constituting a quasi-ballistic missile. This makes predicting its trajectory an impossibility, therefore complicating anti-ballistic missile practices. Furthermore, its depressed trajectory means the missile maintains a higher velocity for the majority of its flight profile, again adding to the difficulty of systems like THAAD to intercept it. Since South Korea has been host to a THAAD battery since late 2017, the showcasing of a system ostensibly tailor-made to counter it can be interpreted as a powerful statement.[68] Nowadays, the Hwasong-11A's wide-scale introduction and its fast response time means that it has often been utilised as a political tool, with launches conducted to match perceived aggressions from the USA and ROK.

A Hwasong-11A is launched on 27 March 2023. Note the rings which held the missile in place falling to the ground in a fashion almost exactly the same as occurs on the Russian 9K720 Iskander(-M), although it is mechanical on that type and pyrotechnic here. The TEL differs substantially from the one seen in the 2018 parade and mirrors contemporary Chinese and Russian TELs such as the MZKT-7930. (KCBC)

The Taebaeksan launcher of the Hwasong-11A missile on parade in early 2018. (KCBC)

The tracked TEL used during the test of 9 May. It joins a rapidly expanding fleet of tracked vehicles available to the MGB. (KCBC)

A Hwasong-11A missile seen prior to launch on 9 May 2019. Although the rear of the missile is highly similar to the 9M723K1 missile, close examination of the various components reveals a range of differences likely explained by indigenous manufacture. (KCBC)

Kim Jong Un tours a storage facility for Hwasong-11As with his daughter Kim Ju Ae in 2022. (KCBC)

A tracked TEL (with a modified cabin design) for the Hwasong-11A during the 75th anniversary of the Workers' Party of Korea parade in 2020. (KCBC)

That the system is intended to expand the KPA's conventional warfighting capabilities as well as its strategic ones is affirmed not only by North Korean press releases, but also by the far-reaching efforts to increase the survivability of its launch platforms. In both 2021 and 2022, a railway-based platform was tested that carried two concealed missiles in an ordinary cargo train wagon, thus expanding the scope of potentially nuclear-capable assets that need to be destroyed during wartime to all components of the North Korean railways. Also in 2021, a Hwasong-11A-derived missile (designated the Hwasong-11S, US DoD designation KN-33) that featured grid fins and a gas ejector enabling cold launch was tested from the North's Gorae-class submarine, indicating the missile may be used from North Korea's next generation of SSBs. A test of the same system the following year was reported to have been conducted from a missile silo installed in an inland reservoir. Though analysts have questioned the utility of this approach, the fact remains that it is both very difficult to locate such facilities and to destroy them, due to the mass of water protecting the silo. A more conventional land-based silo containing a Hwasong-11A was also tested in early 2023, raising the spectre of a North Korean silo-based missile arsenal emerging in the near future. Although this approach technically offers less survivability than a mobile launcher as the silo can be compromised by satellite imagery beforehand, the fact that the DPRK is no longer constrained by the number of TELs it can produce for the deployment of this missile is significant, severely diminishing the prospect of prematurely destroying these assets in a first strike. The Hwasong-11S also appears to be under consideration for fitting to VLS on the Choe Hyon-class destroyers, with the first two ships in the class initially fitted with 10 launch cells for these missiles. However, no tests of the Hwasong-11S from such platforms is known to have occurred, and the lead ship in the class has now been refitted without Hwasong-11S VLS.

A railway-based Hwasong-11A just prior to launch in 2021. The missiles are installed crosswise rather than side-by-side as on its regular chassis. (KCBC)

The lead Choe Hyon-class destroyer was initially fitted with VLS cells for 10 Hwasong-11S', but these were removed during a refit conducted shortly after launch. The missiles' future deployment on the destroyers is uncertain. (KCBC)

A Hwasong-11A is launched from a silo in 2023. This remains the sole such test known to have occurred, and there is no indication a widespread deployment of silo-based Hwasong-11s is occurring. (KCBC)

A Hwasong-11S is test-launched from the modified Gorae-class in 2021. (KCBC)

Aside from introducing new launch platforms, the same missile has also been used as a template for a number of derivatives, together constituting the broader Hwasong-11 missile family. Already in 2019, a system was showcased which mated two shortened Hwasong-11A missiles in square canisters to a tracked platform, producing an aesthetic that was seemingly intentionally reminiscent of the US MGM-140 ATACMS. Using the same engine as the Hwasong-11A but at a length of some 7.1 metres, it is in fact far larger than the (610mm diameter, four metres length) ATACMS, and tests suggest it has a range of greater than 410 kilometres (using a depressed trajectory and late-flight pull-up manoeuvres with an apogee of no more than 50 kilometres), placing it firmly in the SRBM category. The resulting system is known in North Korea as the Hwasong-11Na (Hwasong-11B, US DoD designation KN-24). Curiously, the tracked launcher associated with the system is in fact based on the Chonma/T-62-derived tank line, suggesting that production lines for both tracked platforms exist in parallel and are used as such to speed up production of tracked TELs. To accommodate the still very sizeable missiles, the Chonma chassis was reversed and lengthened by one road wheel. A wheeled TEL of a common design to that used by the Hwasal-1 and 2 cruise missile systems was unveiled only much later, but has since seen significant production as well.

A Hwasong-11B is launched from its canister in August 2019, on a beach near Wonsan. (KCBC)

Kim Jong Un and various individuals involved in the August 2019 test launch stand in front of the tracked TEL used with the system. Note that the perspective used in the image makes the launcher appear somewhat larger than it really is. (KCBC)

Exhibiting a design clearly evocative of the US MGM-140 ATACMS, the Hwasong-11B has been subject to fewer publicised test firings compared to the Hwasong-11A. (KCBC)

Wheeled and tracked launchers of the Hwasong-11B fill a North Korean factory floor in August 2023. (KCBC)

The Hwasong-11B is notable for being the first ballistic missile system confirmed to have been exported by the DPRK since the start of the millennium. In a stunning violation of unilaterally-imposed UN sanctions, Russia in late 2023 took delivery of North Korean SRBMs and utilised them to strike (civilian) targets in Ukraine. The debris of the booster of one such missile landing in front of an apartment complex in the heart of Kharkiv was conclusively matched to footage of Hwasong-11As (and Bs) under assembly in a North Korean facility taken months before. In September of 2024, a photograph of an intact missile that apparently failed and crashed into a field allowed a conclusive identification of the system in question as a Hwasong-11B. Although both the US and Ukraine have claimed prolific use of these missiles started on 30 December, open-source evidence can conclusively verify only limited cases of their use. Moreover, the claims of the latter that out of 50 missiles launched debris of only 21 could be recovered because the remainder veered off course and exploded mid-air seem implausible.[69] Nevertheless, the Kharkiv strike and other confirmed or plausible incidents of Hwasong-11A/B use seem to suggest its accuracy has left much to desire, and the Hwasong-11 family possibly performs poorly in an ECM-heavy environment. Additionally, analysis of its components suggest it lacks the penetration aids of the 9K720 Iskander (whose performance in the Russo-Ukrainian War has been similarly underwhelming), and that its guidance suite is almost entirely composed of Western-acquired electronics.[70] Though the latter illustrates just how easily North Korea can gain access to foreign dual-use components for its ballistic missiles, it also exposes a vulnerability both in terms of allowable production volumes and performance parameters. Its rocky combat-debut notwithstanding, the Hwasong-11A/B was demonstrated as a real and viable combat system both in strategic and conventional scenarios, with production quantities evidently leaving ample space for export despite its recent introduction to the MGB itself. Interestingly, analysis of the components showed many had been manufactured in 2023, with some of the later strikes even producing debris with marks attesting to a build year of 2024.[71] The reason for the use of the Hwasong-11B rather than the Hwasong-11A is likely because the latter's import poses greater logistical challenges, and because the former boasts sufficient range to hit most targets in Ukraine.[72] The deployment provides an obvious opportunity for North Korea

A suspected Hwasong-11B is tested at Russia's Kapustin Yar rocket launch complex in 2023. Curiously, the missile appears to have a modified payload shroud, possibly to enable integration with the Iskander's 9P78-1 TEL. (Russian MoD)

Kim Jong Un tours a facility where close to a hundred Hwasong-11A and Hwasong-11C are being assembled in December 2025. (KCBC)

Kim Jong Un inspects guidance sections of Hwasong-11A missiles under assembly during a visit to their production plant in December 2025. (KCBC)

Debris from the booster section of a North Korean Hwasong-11B that struck the centre of Kharkiv on 2 January 2024. Unlike on the 9K720 Iskander, the Hwasong-11B's warhead separates before impact, thus allowing components of the booster to survive flight largely intact. (© Conflict Armament Research, 2024)

What remains of the guidance section of the Hwasong-11B that struck Kharkiv in early 2024. Of the 290 identified foreign components, over 90 percent were produced in the USA and Europe, the majority in the past three years. (© Conflict Armament Research, 2024)

to assess the effectiveness of its new ballistic missile family and incorporate improvements. Unsurprisingly, reports in early 2025 suggested that North Korean missiles launched since December 2024 boasted improved accuracy under combat conditions of some 50 to 100 metres CEP.[73] The reports coincided with indications that North Korea was developing advanced inertial guidance suite components like fibre-optic gyroscopes with a Russian company, potentially allowing for substantial improvements in accuracy for a range of North Korean weapons systems.[74]

In early 2021, the parade marking the 8th Congress of the Workers' Party of Korea revealed that aside from a shortened Hwasong-11A variant the obverse was also under development. A lengthened missile two of which share the same 10x10 heavy-duty TEL was showcased and successfully tested a few months later, exhibiting a range of at least 600 kilometres with a depressed trajectory that reportedly incorporated irregular (pull-up) flight manoeuvres. The resulting system is known as the Hwasong-11Da (Hwasong-11C, US DoD designation KN-30). Although the missile's extended length may suggest a much longer maximum range (potentially placing it well in the MRBM category), the accompanying news commentary instead suggested that the warhead weight had been increased to 2,500 kilogrammes, likely in a calculated effort to outperform the South's Hyunmoo-4 missile which can carry a maximum of 2,000 kilogrammes in payload.[75] If the commentary was accurate, this would be sufficient for the missile to take out even the most hardened targets and in addition carry sizeable nuclear weapons, while potentially even threatening targets in Japan should it be equipped with smaller payloads like the Hwasan-31 tactical nuclear warhead as well. In early 2024, state media reporting of a test of a 'Hwasongpho-11Da-4.5' variant with a claimed 4,500 kilogrammes warhead unusually came paired with the information that it had been conducted at the type's maximum range of 500 kilometres.[76] The report, which included no images of the system, went on to claim a follow-up test at a range of 250 kilometres would be conducted next July; it instead occurred in September 2024 at a range of 332 kilometres.[77] [78] Although the Hwasong-11C is highly impressive both for its flexibility and surprisingly advanced capabilities, its introduction will be restrained by the amount of 10x10 TELs the DPRK can produce, with TEL production so far seemingly focussing primarily on other missiles in the Hwasong-11 family. If North Korean markings are to be believed, at least 12 TELs enabling the deployment of a total of 24 missiles were introduced by early 2022. There has been some evidence of subsequent continued production, but its rate is thought to be tempered because wheeled heavy TELs (including those for longer-ranged missiles) are assembled in series at the same facility.

Having multiple redundant weapon systems available to strike at the same target helps it retain some of the flexibility typically offered by modern air forces – allowing for the selection of the most cost-effective option for each mission. Yet another new short-range ballistic missile system first showcased and tested in April 2022 would again expand the North's strike options, this time providing a dedicated launch capability in the tactical ballistic missile category. Featuring four missiles in square canisters on a (for North Korean standards surprisingly sensible) 6x6 armoured truck, the Hwasong-11Ra (Hwasong-11D, US DoD designation KN-35) bears some resemblance to the South Korean KTSSM, an ATACMS-inspired weapons system with the express aim of countering North Korean artillery systems. While being much smaller than the conceptually similar Hwasong-11A, the new missile still outsizes the KTSSM a fair bit at an estimated diameter of over 800mm and a length of more than five metres. Its range has so far been confirmed out to about 235 kilometres, and the layout of the Hwasong-11D's cable raceways seems to suggest it can equip a comparatively large payload and guidance section; it is furthermore known to be compatible with the Hwasan-31 tactical nuclear warhead. Although it is certainly a useful addition to its nuclear deterrent and tactical ballistic missile arsenal, perhaps the most significant aspect of this weapon is the fact that it should be cheaper to produce and use

A Hwasong-11C is test-launched in 2021. Note the distinctive paint scheme, and the stylised cabin of the 10x10 TEL. (KCBC)

The effect on target of a Hwasong-11C with a claimed 4,500 kilogramme warhead. Unusually, the target zone was located on a mountaintop roughly 30 kilometres north of the Punggye-ri Nuclear Test Site. Also notable is the fact that the warhead did not separate before impact. (KCBC)

Four members of the Hwasong-11 family displayed side-by-side at the Self-Defence-2021 exhibition. From left to right: The Hwasong-11A, Hwasong-11B, Hwasong-11C, railway-launched Hwasong-11A. (KCBC)

than its larger cousins, raising the spectre of a widespread introduction of tactical ballistic missile systems to the KPA. Such an introduction is exactly what followed only shortly after its first tests. In May 2024, an unprecedented delivery to the MGB of 100 Hwasong-11D missile systems occurred. A test the same month suggested improvements of the missile were ongoing, with state media reports indicating its inertial navigation system guidance had been improved, possibly in response to the poor performance of GNSS-guided Hwasong-11Bs in Ukraine. Things escalated once more in early August the same year, when a stunning ceremony at Pyongyang's Mirim parade training grounds saw 250 Hwasong-11D missile systems (presumably including the 100 finished in May) transferred to frontline units, good for the prompt deployment of 1,000 nuclear-capable tactical ballistic missiles. To remove any doubts about the system's pivotal role in the KPA's future force makeup, state media reports covering the event referred to the weapons as 'new-type tactical ballistic missile launchers to be commissioned as a new core striking weapon of the DPRK armed forces'.[79] In October 2025, the Hwasong-11D also proved part of the weapons options available for a new modular MRL unveiled at the 'Military Hardware Exhibition Defence Development-2025'. The fitting of either one or two missiles in addition to 122mm or 240mm rocket pods reaffirms the ATACMS analogy, and highlights the rapidly growing availability, versatility, and practicality of North Korean short-ranged and tactical ballistic missiles.

Modular multiple rocket launchers pass by during the 80th anniversary of the foundation of the Workers' Party of Korea parade. Appearing to draw inspiration from the US HIMARS, each launcher can carry two pods containing either 36 122mm rockets, nine 240mm rockets, or one Hwasong-11D missile, significantly enhancing their versatility. (KCBC)

An indigenous infantry mobility vehicle patterned after the Komatsu LAV leads a battalion of Hwasong-11D prior to a test in 2022. (KCBC)

Kim Jong Un inspects a warehouse storing 100 Hwasong-11D TELs in May 2024. The accompanying media commentary suggested production of the type was ongoing. (KCBC)

Hundreds of Hwasong-11Ds are displayed in Pyongyang in a nighttime ceremony in August 2024 that gave dystopian science fiction a run for its money. (KCBC)

The Hwasong-11D's 6x6 TEL features a lightly armoured cab, now standard on all new North Korean ballistic missile launchers. Note that on this early test the missile simply breaks through the canister cap, issues with this method meant that the serial production cap opens on a hinge. (KCBC)

In late 2025, a sixth and (so far) final member of the Hwasong-11 family was unveiled. Utilising the Hwasong-11C's lengthened body and engine, the Hwasong-11Ma (Hwasong-11E) swaps its oversized warhead for a large HGV of a design not yet seen on other systems. Like the Hwasong-12B's HGV, it features a flattened underside employed to generate lift, but it does so by the addition of streamlined fins along the length of the warhead rather than the complexly-shaped vehicle employed by the Hwasong-12B, likely in an effort to simplify manufacturing. Two aerodynamic and two guidance fins near the base of the vehicle further distinguish it from earlier HGVs, possibly hinting at an improved understanding of HGV behaviour in hypersonic regimes. Its similarity in this configuration to the YKJ-1000 low-cost hypersonic missile unveiled by the private Chinese company Lingkong Tianxing Technology in November 2025 is rather conspicuous. Given that the Hwasong-11E is a fair bit larger, a direct technological link need not exist, but the possibility of a technology transfer (through cooperation or espionage) cannot be excluded. The first publicised tests followed shortly after its unveiling, with two hypersonic missiles believed to be Hwasong-11Es reportedly launched over a distance of some 400 kilometres in October 2025. In January 2026, the HGV's characteristics were put to the test, with another two launches believed to involve Hwasong-11Es striking a simulated target in the ocean at a distance of approximately 1,000 kilometres using a boost-skip manoeuvre. Telemetry photographed during the event suggested a depressed trajectory with a maximum altitude of 74.3 kilometres (possibly to reduce peak stresses on the HGV), and a maximum speed of 3,732 metres per second (close to Mach 11). Given that South Korea's Joint Chiefs of Staff (JCS) claimed similar ranges of 900 and 950 kilometres for this test, the initial survival of the HGVs following the manoeuvre can be tentatively confirmed. On a more efficient trajectory, regional targets such as Japan are believed to be in range. With two missiles fitted to a (by North Korean standards) fairly compact vehicle, this would provide the DPRK with a regional nuclear deterrent that is highly survivable both before and after launch. Moreover, the system may provide an answer to the failure of Hwasong-11 type missiles to penetrate defences during the Ukraine War, thus allowing it to more convincingly take out systems like THAAD and Patriot.

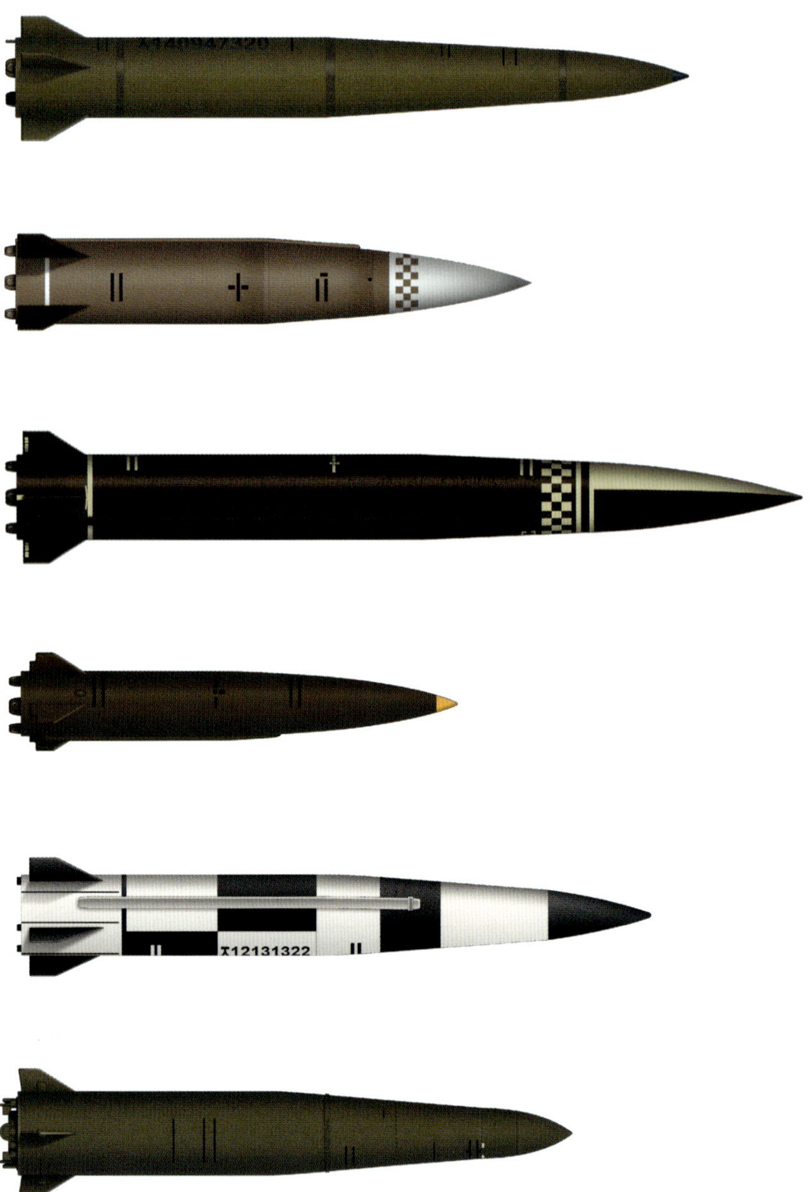

The (non-HGV part of the) Hwasong-11 missile family, depicting from top to bottom the Hwasong-11A, Hwasong-11B, Hwasong-11C, Hwasong-11D and Hwasong-11S at the same scale. For comparison, a Russian 9K720 was added to scale at the bottom. (Artwork by Anderson Subtil)

In just half a decade, the new solid-fuelled SRBM family has transmogrified the North's short-ranged arsenal beyond what anyone could have expected. Where at the start of the century the DPRK was largely reliant upon Scud-derived missile systems, which require highly specialised training, lengthy fuelling, and are comparatively easy to shoot down, it can now call on scores of missiles that have larger range, are potentially capable of attaining high accuracies and are featured in pairs or even quadruples on each launcher. Development of new variants in the family as well as the rate of introduction if anything is seemingly speeding up, to the point where North Korea's moratorium on ballistic missile exports has finally been broken once more. The Hwasong-11 missile family's advent showcases perhaps like no other example how quickly a threat can evolve if left unchecked.

The diverse mass of new missile systems with overlapping roles being introduced to the KPA is reflective not only of the gradual and experimental nature of the North's missile programme, but also of its intention to introduce a large variety of striking options for each potential target, almost to the point of supplanting the Air Force in this role. This goal was further underlined by yet another addition to the DPRK's long-ranged striking capabilities first tested in the summer of 2019. Uncomfortably perched between a true ballistic missile system and an MRL, the massive new device (US DoD designation KN-25) was first tested in late July, twice again in August,

Hwasong-11Es showcased during the 2025 parade celebrating the 80th anniversary of the founding of the WPK. The TEL is the same one also used by the Hwasong-11C. (KCBC)

and once more in September that year. The rockets are 600mm in diameter and about eight metres in length, contributing to an estimated weight of some 3.5 tonnes. This earns the various launchers (all apparently collectively designated merely as '600mm Super/Ultra-Large MRLs') the technical distinction of being the largest tubed MRLs in existence. One of the key difficulties in producing such large-calibre MRLs is that spin stabilisation of a rocket that size is infeasible – with SRBMs typically using sophisticated guidance suites, aerodynamic fins and very different aspect ratios to mitigate this issue. North Korea came up with its own unique solution however, introducing a rotating section at the rear of the rocket with foldable fins that provides a measure of spin stabilisation. This has the additional benefit of allowing the missile's sensitive guidance suite to remain oriented in the same direction, allowing it to achieve high accuracy, especially when used in conjunction with GNSS guidance. Consequently, a high rate of reliability and CEP on the order of tens of metres (in a test setting) can be achieved. The newest variant, first tested in January 2026, reportedly replaced such guidance with a fully inertial suite.[80] While eliminating opportunities for jamming or spoofing, inertial guidance suites typically attain lower accuracy due to the accumulation of error by its gyroscopes and other inertial measurement sensors. The accompanying imagery of this launch showcased an accuracy comparable to the GNSS variant however, thus suggesting significant advances in the development of such sensors have occurred.

The weapon's first tests utilised a depressed trajectory with an apogee of below 30 kilometres and therefore reached a range of only 250 kilometres, which is not much greater than the range attained by the North's much smaller 300mm MRL, albeit doing so at an unusually high velocity of Mach 6.5. Later tests would prove the system's abilities further, attaining a range of up to 400 kilometres when fired on a more conventional ballistic trajectory with an apogee of 100 kilometres. The maximum range, as attested by North Korean statements, is 420 kilometres. This enables it to strike at targets in the South from deep within the DPRK and brings almost the whole of South Korea into range when deployed closer to the front lines. Although it may therefore comfortably be called an SRBM, there is actually some contention about whether the system is operated by the MGB or also the KPA's ground forces branch – with only the former confirmed. In this capacity, the DPRK has claimed it can be used to deploy tactical nuclear warheads, underlining its claims regarding the mass production of miniaturised nuclear weapons. The method of operation is also closer to a ballistic missile than an MRL, with the missile's size making field reloads impractical. Instead, missiles are sealed in their tubes in the factory, and the tubes are believed to be replaced as a whole at supply depots. The very high launch cadence of this missile system means that it can be considered among the more reliable in North Korean service, and makes it partially responsible for the sharp uptick in North Korean ballistic missile tests in recent years.

Five very different TELs have been developed for this system so far, each capable of carrying a different number of missiles. The first, apparently based on the same Songun-derived chassis used for the Kumsong-3 coastal defence system, carries just three missiles side-by-side in square canisters which extend far past the TEL's front, and seems to have been used for initial testing only. The second and largest utilised a new Songun-derived chassis with 10 road wheels on either side, allowing it to carry six tubes in a 2x3 configuration; this tracked TEL is larger even than the one used for the Pukguksong-2 MRBM. The third launch introduced yet another new large wheeled 4x4 TEL carrying four missiles in a 2x2 configuration. Tellingly,

A Hwasong-11E displayed at the 'Military Hardware Exhibition Defence Development-2025', providing a good look at its HGV. (KCBC)

whereas the first two launches from tracked TELs were conducted from rural areas, the third and fourth were from hardened airfields, underscoring the differences in utility each platform offers. Finally, in 2024 a fourth platform was added utilising the same MZKT-7930-like 8x8 TEL that is also used to carry two Hwasong-11A ballistic missiles, underscoring just how large the 600mm MRL is. A fifth platform unveiled at the 'National Defence Development-2024' exhibition the same year retained the same 8x8 chassis, but modified the armoured cabin to resemble that of the US HIMARS. The same platform was iterated upon over 2025, with parade examples first displaying six missiles in a slightly staggered arrangement, before a final variant with just five missiles was unveiled during an inspection by Kim Jong Un of a production facility at the end of the year.

Although procuring suitable TELs may remain a difficulty, the fact that new types are continually being designed and built shows that the DPRK is serious about introducing these new missile systems in large numbers. This fact was underlined by a delivery of 30 of the six-tubed tracked launchers on the last day of 2022, which was accompanied by the statement that 'the relevant complex… …assembled one, even two, gigantic units in addition every two days'. Such a production rate might seem implausible (and could indeed refer only to assembly of partially finished products), yet the total number of launchers spotted so far with unique markings is in excess of 70, which is sufficient to allow the deployment of over 400 of these new potentially nuclear-capable SRBMs. In reality, the numbers introduced so far are likely to substantially exceed these figures, with a single mass-fire demonstration in May 2024 featuring 18 launchers together capable of launching 96 missiles. Supposedly, this demonstration was conducted by the 3rd Battalion of the 331st Red Artillery Regiment – implying a single MGB SRBM regiment

The tracked 600mm MRL during a test in 2020. (KCBC)

A delivery ceremony of tracked 600mm MRLs at the end of 2022, showcasing the unprecedented size of its TEL. (KCBC)

Eighteen 600mm MRLs, of which 12 of the tracked variant and the others wheeled, line up at Pyongyang Sunan prior to a May 2024 firepower demonstration. (KCBC)

The May 2024 eighteen-tuple launch. The apparent deviation from their course of some of the missiles was likely corrected in flight, and the target was struck with remarkable accuracy from 365 kilometres distance. (KCBC)

Above: A new MZKT-7930-like 8x8 wheeled TEL for the 600mm MRL during a test firing in September 2024. (KCBC)

Left: Yet another new wheeled 8x8 TEL reminiscent of the HIMARS's FMTV M1140 at the National Defence Development-2024 exhibition. (KCBC)

Below: Kim Jong Un inspects at least 19 five-tube 600mm MRLs under assembly in late 2025. Though the TEL is similar to the six-tube variant, it is slightly shorter. (KCBC)

might have control of over 300 missiles. Most other nations have thus far eschewed introducing extremely large-calibre MRLs due to the high costs involved and a perceived lack of novel capabilities, but to North Korea these systems are essential to fill in the gaps left by an ageing fleet of aircraft. The adoption of the 600mm MRLs has therefore been as enthusiastic as that of the Hwasong-11 missile family, and a variety of different warheads are known to be associated with the JBT-6 missile used by the system.[81] This is thought to include cluster, HE, and thermobaric warheads, aside from tactical nuclear warheads that can be utilised in an airburst mode. The 600mm system's success was underwritten by statements by Kim Jong Un in late 2025 that it 'will be the main strike means of the KPA' and 'would completely change the composition of our artillery force'.[82] Whether it will indeed supplant legacy artillery remains to be seen, but it is clear that North Korea's SRBM successes are of profound consequence to its other military branches as well.

To better describe the most recent developments in large solid-fuelled ballistic missiles, we must turn back time half a decade or more to acknowledge some telling early signs of sinister future developments. The direction in which the North Korean strategic ballistic missile programme was heading by the end of the 2010s was ambitious and broad-ranging, and the way to several advanced and potentially severely destabilising technologies lay wide open. The most openly hinted future development was clearly showcased during the parade for the 105th anniversary of Kim Il Sung's birthday in 2017, where two canister-based designs were shown that when tested could well have ranges that put them in the IRBM/ICBM classification. As obvious offshoots of the Pukguksong solid-fuelled ballistic missile family, they represented the DPRK's first efforts towards producing a fully reliable solid-fuelled ICBM that can be fired in a moment's notice: comparable to such systems as the Russian RT-2PM2 Topol-M which is considered a very potent

One of two canister-based ICBM prototypes showcased during the 105th anniversary of Kim Il Sung's birthday parade of 2017. The use of these modified WS51200 TE(L)s is notable, as all (with the possible exception of one) were later modified to carry the Hwasong-15. (KCBC)

The second canister-based ICBM prototype. Based on a flatbed truck, this configuration will be much easier to produce in numbers for the DPRK. Although both canisters are very dissimilar, they may in fact represent the same solid-fuelled ICBM programme. (NK Pro)

nuclear deterrent. As most technologies that enable the production of such systems, such as fibre-wound casings, gas generators for cold launches and other technologies shared by liquid-fuelled ICBMs, had readily been tested, the main hurdle would consist of essentially scaling up existing designs. It is no coincidence then that one of the two designs displayed, at the time based on five modified WS51200 16x12 TELs which are now used for the Hwasong-15, bore significant similarity to the Pukguksong-2, the main difference being a massive increase in length to roughly 20 metres. The second canister shown is of comparable size, yet not design, but acknowledges the fact that TELs such as the WS51200 remained scarce by utilising a modified flatbed truck as its TE(L). Although this limits this design to the use of highways and large paved roads, thereby greatly diminishing its ability to hide from foreign reconnaissance during wartime, it would allow for a greater production run – in turn counteracting the loss in functionality.

The missiles that might have been destined for the launchers paraded in 2017 were never tested, and the WS51200s were soon repurposed to carry the Hwasong-15. In this sense, their participation in the parade is likely to have been largely symbolic, serving both as a propaganda tool and to highlight the existence of a solid-fuelled ICBM programme. It was not until December 2022 that the next indication came that this programme was still advancing, when North Korea tested a solid-fuel rocket motor at the Sohae Satellite Launching Ground that was reportedly capable of attaining a thrust of 140 metric tonnes. With the diameter of the test tank housing the engine measuring close to two metres, there was little doubt that this engine was destined for use on an ICBM class design. The 140 metric tonnes of thrust is equally notable however, as it implied an engine that is significantly more powerful than the ones used for comparable systems abroad. Shortly thereafter, during the parade celebrating the 75th anniversary of the foundation of the Korean People's Army in February 2023, a first look was granted at what had become of North Korea's solid-fuelled ICBM ambitions. Five of the now lengthened WS51200 TELs were overhauled once more to carry the gigantic canisters that would during operational deployment house a lethal delivery system and payload. Although the missiles remained concealed until a first test launch, the launchers and their canisters settled into a more plausible-looking configuration, with certain external characteristics especially of the Russian RS-24 Yars seemingly having been copied over to the North Korean design. The first test launch came only shortly thereafter in April 2023, followed by two more later that year. Each was intentionally limited in its range, adjusting the apogee to at most 6,648.4 kilometres (for the second test in July) to fly a ground distance of approximately 1,000 kilometres by firing the second and third stages oriented upwards. This performance exceeds the parameters demonstrated for North Korea's liquid-fuelled ICBM tests fired on a similarly lofted trajectory, and suggests that the new ICBM, which was announced to the world as the Hwasong-18, can comfortably strike targets as far as 15,000 kilometres away. The missile itself has a clear design debt to the Russian Topol-M or Yars road-mobile ICBMs, featuring three stages all thought to be powered by solid-fuelled engines, with the first stage significantly wider than the second and third. Despite these global similarities in both launch vehicle, missile, and its method of operation, it is unlikely that there is any direct technological link. Not only has North Korea's gradual accession to these technologies been well-documented, the Hwasong-18 is also substantially more compact than either the Topol-M and Yars. With a diameter of some 1.7 metres for the first stage and a length of a little over 20 metres, it falls short of both their length and width. Some have further suggested that the lack of an external gyrocompass like the ones on Russian equivalent systems suggests the DPRK utilises a more time-consuming laser-based method to align its launcher.[83] While this may well be correct, it should be noted that the period between set-up and launch observed during test launches seemed to be notably short. For the time being, the Hwasong-18 seems to constitute an actual end product for North Korea's road-mobile ICBM programme rather than yet another developmental step, with state media describing it as 'the core weapon system of the strategic force of the Democratic People's Republic of Korea'.

The choice of the WS51200-derived TEL was in this context questionable, as it limited the system to a maximum of six operationally deployed ICBMs at any given time. While this might have been sufficient for systems that in retrospect seem to have been little more than developmental stepping stones, North Korea soon

The claimed 140 metric tonnes thrust solid-fuelled engine after testing in December 2022, which reportedly included a test of its thrust-vector controlling technology. (KCBC)

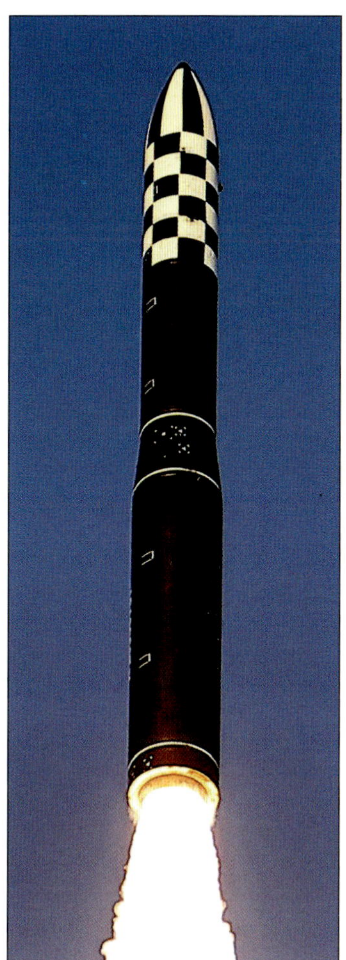

A Hwasong-18 in flight during its third test flight, showing clearly the massive solid-fuelled engine's nozzle. Gimballing appears to be used for steering. (KCBC)

MGB personnel prepare a Hwasong-18 before its first test launch in April 2023. The unit involved in the test was reported as a 'Second Red Flag' Company. (KCBC)

Seemingly seeking to highlight the ability of the Hwasong-18 to utilise civilian infrastructure to hide from prying eyes, at least two of its tests saw the launcher emerge from highway tunnels. (KCBC)

demonstrated it held more lofty ambitions for the Hwasong-18. In coverage of a TEL production facility in January and May 2024, a new indigenous TEL was displayed that would help to finally unshackle it from its made-in-China chains. Though it is largely similar to the WS51200 18x12 TEL in terms of its length, cab, chassis and wheels, the vehicle is significantly wider, allowing the missile canister to be recessed further into the body resulting in a less top-heavy design. It appears to be powered by a tank engine, possibly a derivative of the 780 horsepower V-46 used by the T-72, which should offer comparable performance to the WS51200's original German engine. While this allows some mobility on rough terrain, that it is not an off-road vehicle was attested by the use of prepared launch sites during testing.[84] The introduction of Hwasong-18 variants on indigenous TELs marks the first time North Korea can field an ICBM that is not vulnerable either due to the limited number of platforms available, or due to being subject to lengthy fuelling before launch.

The Hwasong-18, for its (relative) compactness, quick deployment time, and adequate payload capabilities, makes for a sensible compromise between size and practicality, and thus constitutes a suitable centrepiece for a country's road-mobile deterrent. Of course, North Korea is known for anything but its willingness to compromise. Little more than a year and a half after the Hwasong-18's inaugural flight, the Hwasong-19 attained the same stage of development – once more without any indication of it even existing beforehand. First launched on 31 October 2024, it once again pushed the boundaries for North Korean ICBM performance, tracing a lofted trajectory that took its payload to an altitude of 7,687.5 kilometres before impacting the ocean at a distance of 1,001.2 kilometres after a flight of a little under 86 minutes. On a regular trajectory, this would be sufficient to strike any target of choice on the globe, although precise payload characteristics for

The Hwasong-18's third test was conducted from an inconspicuous country road. Note the mechanism introduced to keep the nose of the canister from falling to the ground and getting damaged. (KCBC)

Kim Jong Un tours a warehouse in May 2024 where the six converted WS51200 TELs, eight Hwasong-17 TELs and two new-production Hwasong-18 TELs are stored (in addition to a wheeled TEL for the 600mm MRL). In an adjacent facility, 11 more TELs for the Hwasong-18 were under construction at that time. (KCBC)

the moment remain a mystery. To achieve this feat, a new first stage engine was developed, increasing its diameter to approximately 2.4 metres. The testing campaign for the engine was quite extensive and in fact continued after the Hwasong-19's first and only launch, with eight tests reportedly conducted by September 2025. Shockingly, the thrust developed by this engine was claimed to be 200 metric tonnes, implying a missile weight that exceeds that of any other foreign road-mobile ICBM, including the Chinese DF-41/61.[85] Like the Hwasong-18, The Hwasong-19 is composed of three stages, with the second and third shrinking to approximately two metres in diameter, resulting in a total length of some 26.5 metres (including the gas generator). Interestingly, the Hwasong-19 appears to use fibre-wound casings for its propellant tanks to save weight, a feature which was not evident on the Hwasong-18. Notable in test footage is the presence of an apparent post-boost vehicle (PBV), featuring a dual rocket engine that is used to accurately propel a payload bus towards its target. A diagram displayed at the National Defence Development-2024 exhibition gave an indication of the intended payload, with either a large solitary re-entry vehicle or seven MIRVs capable of being fitted in the shroud. However, an actual deployment of a MIRV payload during testing does not appear to have occurred. The 22x20 TEL used to deploy this latest gargantuan is an offshoot of the Hwasong-17's, featuring 11 axles on an extra-wide chassis over 30 metres in length that was first inspected by Kim Jong Un in early September 2024.[86]

Being just the latest road-mobile ICBM in a rather baffling series of six or more entirely distinct ICBM designs unveiled in little more than a decade, the Hwasong-19 cautions the analyst against declaring a finalised form for its ICBM programme. There are some grounded reasons to suspect this is in fact the case however, with North Korean state media quoting Kim Jong Un as stating the Hwasong-19 is 'the perfected weapon system of ICBM Hwasongpho-19, to be used by the strategic forces of the DPRK along with Hwasongpho-18'.[87] Moreover, the system's form factor as a very heavy, MIRV-capable, solid-fuelled and road-mobile ICBM seems to approach a clear point of diminishing returns for further growth. Consolidation around this design would present the Missile General Bureau with a formidable strategic delivery system, while allowing North Korean developmental efforts to refocus on its myriad other modern weapons programmes. And

Kim Jong Un attends the deployment of the Hwasong-19 ICBM before its inaugural launch in October 2024. (KCBC)

The 'Second Red Flag' Company involved in the launch during preparations. Note the erection mechanism's gigantic telescopic hydraulic cylinders, easily eight metres in length. (KCBC)

The Hwasong-19 during its first test firing in October 2024. Note that the (disguised) pre-prepared hardened launch pad from the Hwasong-18's testing campaign was used once again. (KCBC)

The Hwasong-19 alongside its monstrous TEL at the National Defence Development-2024 exhibition. Note the payload shroud straddling the PBV which features thrusters for fine course adjustments (KCBC)

indeed, there are indications that future development is not aimed at further missile growth. In September 2025, a visit by Kim Jong Un to the development site of the Hwasong-20 ICBM came paired with commentary suggesting it shared the same 200 metric tonnes force engine. The accompanying imagery likewise showed a reduction in diameter for the second or third stage, restricting the space of possible designs to something fairly close to the Hwasong-19 itself. Interestingly, the 'Military Hardware Exhibition Defence Development-2025' featured what appeared to be a Hwasong-19 with a redesigned payload shroud, seemingly optimised for volume rather than aerodynamics, and omitting the side thrusters believed to be associated with the PBV. Moreover, the hydraulic arms responsible for erecting the missile tube were conspicuously missing, perhaps replaced by a different mechanism obscured within the vehicle itself. It is currently unclear if this design is meant to merely represent a modification of the Hwasong-19 design, or if it in fact constitutes the Hwasong-20. Likewise, it is unclear exactly for which capabilities the modifications are optimising.

A view of the Hwasong-19 in flight shortly after third stage separation, showing the two engine nozzles of the PBV as well as the discarded third stage. (KCBC)

While the Hwasong-19 and Hwasong-20 seemingly mark the end station for North Korea's solid-fuelled, road-mobile ICBM programme, it would be a mistake to think its hunger for ever more and ever newer ballistic missiles was thereby stilled. The observant reader may have noticed the apparent lack of a Hwasong-16 entry in this sprawling missile family, and indeed the DPRK soon got to work to fill the gap. Once more, the first indications that a programme to develop a new missile was underway came from engine tests at its Sohae Satellite Launching Ground. In November 2023 and again in March 2024, North Korean state media reported on tests of a new engine for a solid-fuelled IRBM. While it may be tempting to assume that the engine developed for the Hwasong-18 would suffice for this missile as well, like RD-250-derived engines managed to power most of its modern liquid-fuelled arsenal from IRBM to ICBM, the situation for solid-fuelled missiles is markedly different. Rather than igniting in the combustion chamber, in solid-fuelled missiles the propellant is lit in the centre of the stage along its entire length, so that the thrust produced (and consequently the required design specifications) depends on the exact dimensions of the stage. Confusingly, while the ground test campaign was still ongoing, the first complete article was already tested in January 2024. Coverage of the test was brief, keeping

Kim Jong Un inspects a suspected Hwasong-20 ICBM at the General Academy of Chemical Materials in September 2025. The paint scheme is distinct from either known Hwasong-19 variant. (KCBC)

A modified Hwasong-19 or Hwasong-20 is displayed at the 'Military Hardware Exhibition Defence Development-2025' in October 2025. Note the absence of hydraulics to erect the missile tube, and the rounded payload shroud. (KCBC)

the missile unnamed and referencing only its status as an IRBM, with a photo of the launch showing it to be a two-staged design. Though its precise dimensions remain uncertain, the diameter is estimated to be close to 1.6 metres, with the missile's total length not exceeding 22 metres (of which about six metres taken up by the glider). The design is thus similar in size to the liquid-fuelled Hwasong-12, and in fact used its TEL for early tests. Estimates of the missile's range varied significantly, with South Korea claiming a splashdown of its payload at sea after flying 1,000 kilometres while the Japanese reported a range of 500 kilometres, with a maximum altitude of 50 kilometres.[88] The discrepancy was likely caused by the payload involved: commentary referred to a hypersonic manoeuvrable controlled warhead, which imagery showed to be of the same type of HGV tested from an unnamed liquid-fuelled missile in January 2022 (believed perhaps to be the Hwasong-8). While no further tests of the system occurred as of mid-2024, and even the associated TEL is currently unknown, a test of another missile in April 2024 soon provided more clarity. Described as the Hwasong-16Na (Hwasong-16B), this IRBM appears to be identical to the one tested just months prior (consequently believed to be the Hwasong-16A) save for its paint scheme and payload. The payload was once again familiar: though featuring small adjustments in its precise shape, it is largely identical to the Hwasong-12B HGV tested in September 2021. Reporting on its performance also differed significantly again, with South Korea reporting a range of 600 kilometres, Japan 650 kilometres and a maximum altitude of 100 kilometres, and North Korea itself claiming a 1,000 kilometre flight with a double apogee of 101.1 and 72.3 kilometres.[89 90] A similar story developed after a second test in January 2025, with North Korea claiming a 1,500 kilometre flight (with double apogees at 99.8 and 42.5 kilometres) whereas South Korea and Japan both suggested failure after 1,100 kilometres instead.[91] Though it remains difficult to assess this situation because it can be notoriously hard to get an accurate reading of the trajectory of hypersonic missiles, it is evident that the DPRK is still persevering in its HGV testing campaign commenced so intermittently in the 2020s. That it is indeed committed to gaining accurate data of its tests is underlined by the development of a data transceiver marketed by Glocom, which is claimed to 'keep communication performance at hypersonic speeds'.[92] Ongoing improvements of the Hwasong-16B are evident not only in the increased range demonstrated, but also in the claim that 'composite carbon fiber material was used in the manufacture of the engine body'.[93] The amount of resources now invested in the development of HGVs is remarkable, especially considering the uncertainty of success and the relatively marginal performative gains offered by HGVs – with range and payload significantly reduced in exchange for increased survivability, which could also be achieved by simply increasing production volume. Of course, part of the explanation may lie in the prestige gained by becoming one of only a handful of nations to operationally deploy HGVs. To carry the Hwasong-16B, a dedicated new 12x14 TEL was developed, sharing a similar construction and cabin with the WS51200-derived TEL used for the Hwasong-18.

With 20 TELs confirmed available for the Hwasong-17, a further 19 for the Hwasong-18, and at least one for the Hwasong-19, North Korea might soon be able to field at least 40 road-mobile ICBMs, not counting untested alternative launch platforms. Another method of building a credible nuclear deterrence does not rely on mobile launchers at all however, instead concealing ballistic missiles in stationary launch silos across a nation. Even when these have been identified, the fact that launch preparations cannot be detected in advance means they can be highly effective in a first strike. As they are hardened and usually very well hidden, even in a second strike capacity they offer some limited capabilities. Furthermore, since they are not encumbered by the carrying capacity of whatever size TE(L) is available, much heavier designs are possible with greater payloads and generally much more favourable characteristics. The additional costs of building a launch silo can be high, but since acquiring massive TE(L)s and the hydraulics required to erect them is also

The only publicised image of the unnamed solid-fuelled IRBM with HGV payload tested in January 2024. (KCBC)

The Hwasong-16B in flight, showing its first stage engine nozzle. The proportions of the stages match that of the tentative Hwasong-16A. (KCBC)

The Hwasong-16B prior to launch in April 2024, showing clearly its HGV payload and new 12x14 TEL. (KCBC)

The Hwasong-16B prior to testing in April 2024. The launching area is the same prepared location used twice for the Hwasong-18, and once for the tentative Hwasong-16A. (KCBC)

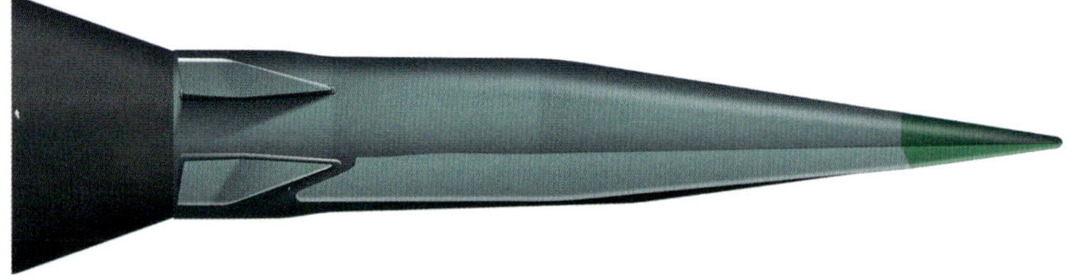

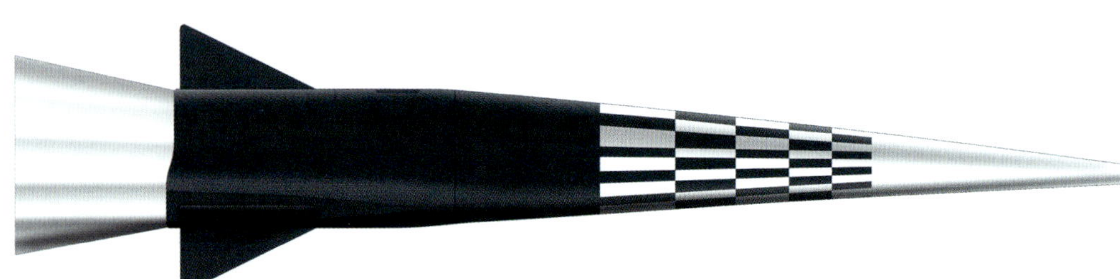

The three models of HGV so far unveiled at the same scale, depicted here with the paint schemes displayed during 2024 and 2025. Note the differences in the designs, with the simple nosecone with fins of the (tentative) Hwasong-12/16A (top) constituting the simplest approach whereas the sleek design of the Hwasong-12/16B's HGV (middle) probably offers increased performance while complicating production. The Hwasong-11E's slightly smaller HGV (bottom) likely strikes a balance between the two approaches. (Artwork by Anderson Subtil)

Left: An early image of a Hwasong-10 TEL moving out of its bunker. Such hardened bases are scattered across the DPRK, and for their simplicity can be very hard to detect. (KCBC)

Below: A Hwasong-11A is launched from its silo in the only such test in 2023. (KCBC)

Kim Jong Un inspects an underground strategic missile base in October 2024. (KCBC)

expensive the trade-off might well be deemed acceptable. Other hardened storage sites for ballistic missiles on TE(L)s are already scattered across the DPRK, with some facilities believed to run below mountains for hundreds of metres. However, these serve merely as hardened bunkers from which mobile ballistic missiles disperse once the order to launch has been given. While no actual launch silos other than the experimental KN-23 SRBM silos have been identified in the DPRK, they represent a plausible and viable future development both for existing missile designs and larger ones that have yet to be developed. For the moment however, it appears North Korea is instead opting for the use of hardened launch facilities from which road-mobile systems are then dispersed. Up to 20 such bases, each containing extensive underground facilities and support structures, are believed to exist within the country.[94] That their use remained a priority was affirmed in October 2024, when Kim Jong Un reportedly toured such facilities and called for their continued fortification and modernisation.[95]

Other Delivery Systems

The start of the 2020s marked the implementation of a nuclear weapons policy that saw the claimed introduction of tactical nuclear warheads to a disturbingly wide range of weapons systems. Although ballistic missiles are and will likely always remain the preferred delivery system, North Korea has invested substantial resources into exploring other avenues of approach. One particularly high profile result of this policy has been the debut of its Hwasal-1 and Hwasal-2 ground-launched cruise missiles (GLCMs), which saw a rigorous testing regime since they were unveiled in 2021. Despite the uncommonly detailed coverage of these tests and the precise parameters involved, the exact role of the two designs remains unclear. What is known is that they constitute large, strategic range cruise missiles with a diameter of approximately 550mm and a length of a little under nine metres (seven without the booster), utilising a booster for launch after which a turbofan engine takes over for cruise flight. Two foldout wings provide control, and terminal guidance can optionally be achieved by a nose-mounted optical sensor. The main difference between the two (aside from usually sporting a contrasting white or black paint coat) appears to be inlet for the turbofan engine, which is much longer and more pronounced on the Hwasal-2 than on the Hwasal-1. Furthermore, the Hwasal-1 appears to include an inertial guidance section after the warhead whereas the Hwasal-2 does not. Nevertheless, there is little discernible difference in performance, with both types attaining a speed of just over 700 kilometres per hour and the Hwasal-1 having a range of at least 1,587 kilometres, and the Hwasal-2 2,000 kilometres. Analysis is complicated by the fact that foreign radar detection of these missiles has been spotty, and because they fly in figure eight patterns during tests to avoid crossing into foreign territory no objective measurements of their characteristics can be made. However, suggestions that the variant with the elongated inlet is an improvement over the other seem to overlook that both were used during the first publicised tests on 11 and 12 September 2021. Matters are complicated further by the fact that both types come in variants with a conventional warhead and TV guidance, as well as variants with tactical nuclear warheads or 'super-large' warheads.[96] Although TV guidance for the latter variants should be mostly redundant, an inspection by Kim Jong Un of supposed Hwasan-31 nuclear warheads in March 2023 also showed a Hwasal-2 that did feature such guidance. While TV guidance could be employed simply to achieve high accuracy in the conventional land attack mode, it is possible the system is also intended for use as an anti-ship missile (AShM), for which its payload would be relatively light and the missile easy to intercept however. Nevertheless, the technologies incorporated in the Hwasal-1 and Hwasal-2 will certainly be appreciated in other branches of the KPA, with the turbofan engines in particular potentially useful to power UAVs. There is no direct information on what engine in particular is used, but with the Kh-35's R95-300 available it seems like a sensible choice, especially given the fact that the same engine gave rise to the conceptually similar Kh-55. With Kim Jong Un inspecting what appeared to be a copy of the more modern Russian TRDD-50A turbofan in 2023, it is possible that engine is utilised instead (or both, if parallel production lines exist), or that it will be incorporated on future production runs.

By virtue of the missile's large size and the fact that five launch canisters are present on each vehicle, the TEL on which they are based is of yet another very large and presumably difficult to produce 8x8 design. Curiously, this new vehicle bears significant similarity to the US M977 HEMTT, possibly arising from an order to replicate a comparable asset in North Korean service. Although a very similar cabin is employed by the 6x6 truck that tows the DPRK's newest strategic surface-to-air missile (SAM) system, that vehicle is believed to have a significantly different design origin. Both the Hwasal-1 and Hwasal-2 appear to use the same launch vehicle, although it is uncertain whether a mixed loadout can be carried. Aside from land-based launch platforms, Hwasal family cruise missiles have also been deployed from North Korea's new Tuman and Amnok class corvettes. Moreover, in January 2025 a cold-launched modification was reportedly demonstrated to the same 1,500 kilometres range as the Hwasal-1, albeit with an engine inlet recessed even further into the missile's body than the Hwasal-2's. The type's designation is unknown, but it was later unveiled to be part of the VLS arsenal of the new Choe Hyon-class destroyers. Also part of the available armament of these new naval assets are three offshoots of the Hwasal family that appear to have been optimised for an AShM role. These consist of a supersonic variant, as well as two downsized variants also of a normal subsonic and supersonic type. Given that these cruise missiles have not yet been ascribed a strategic role, they are covered to greater detail in the previous volume of this series. However, the existence of Hwasals in KPAN service suggests its deployment to branches other than the MGB, and indeed its operational service with the KPAAF is also confirmed.

Aside from the GLCM variants, another cruise missile derived from the same system can be launched from submerged platforms like the Gorae-class SSB, making it a submarine-launched cruise missile (SLCM). Known as the Pulhwasal-3,[97] it was first unveiled during a test in early 2023. The cruise missile seems largely identical to the Hwasal-1 and Hwasal-2, but first introduced the more recessed engine inlet of the VLS-launched Hwasal presumably to make it compatible with a torpedo tube launch mode. Other identifiable characteristics include an all-white paint scheme, slightly shorter stub

The Hwasal-1 strategic cruise missile. Note the large engine inlet. (KCBC)

A Hwasal-2 detonates its warhead over an island during a test in September 2023, simulating a nuclear airburst. (KCBC)

Kim Jong Un tours a display showcasing weapons systems capable of carrying tactical nuclear warheads in March 2023. Note the optical sensor on this Hwasal-1. (KCBC)

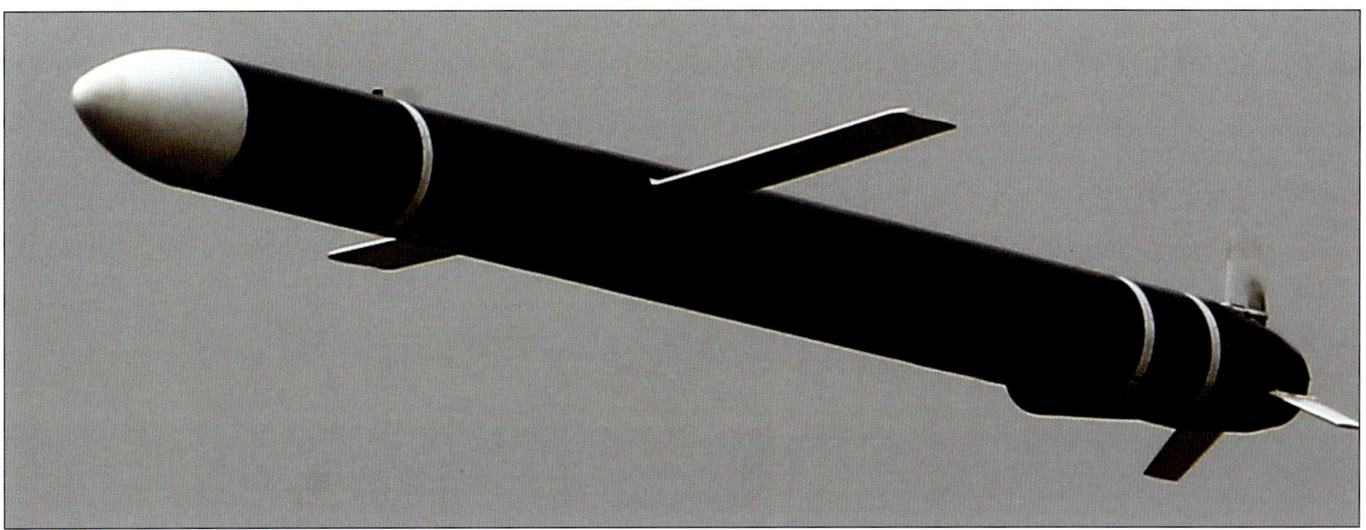

The Hwasal-2 strategic cruise missile. Aside from possibly boasting slightly longer range and a different paint scheme, the engine inlet is different and the guidance section is smaller. (KCBC)

A Hwasal-1 is launched from its 8x8 TEL during tests in early 2023. (KCBC)

wings and a modified booster. To allow its deployment from torpedo tubes, a protective shell containing the missile is ejected from the water, after which the missile's booster engages, in a process similar to that of the French MdCN or Russian Kalibr SLCMs. Given that the Pulhwasal-3 shares the Hwasal-1 and Hwasal-2's approximate size however, it should be too large to be launched from a standard 533mm torpedo tube, necessitating specialised torpedo tubes to be fitted to North Korea's submarine fleet to allow them to deploy this potentially very effective weapon. Reporting of a Pulhwasal-3-31 variant furthermore suggests that it too can utilise the Hwasan-31 tactical nuclear warhead. With their long range (claimed to be at least 1,500 kilometres) and very low demonstrated flight altitude, the Pulhwasal-3 could be a potent first strike weapon against regional targets including Japan and Taiwan, with effective networks of air-defence systems required to reliably shoot them down. Combined with (satellite) reconnaissance, such weapons when equipped with nuclear warheads could even be used against US carrier groups, for the first time providing the DPRK with a plausible deterrent against such well-defended formations.

Having successfully tapped the pool of novel capabilities offered by strategic GLCMs, it is unlikely that North Korea will be content even with the surprisingly powerful systems it has yet demonstrated.

And indeed, another potential GLCM design has been featured in parades since the 75th anniversary of the Workers' Party of Korea parade in 2020 without its missiles ever being tested or displayed. Consequently, all that can be ascertained is that the system consists of four launch tubes almost 10 metres in length, and approximately 700mm in diameter, placed on a flatbed with dedicated launch cabin that is towed by the same 6x6 truck used for the new 9K330 Tor-inspired SAM. While the vehicle was never since spotted during any launches of any of the Hwasal types mentioned above, the fact that it represents a genuine development programme was attested by the showcasing of a significantly reworked launcher at the National Defence Development-2024 exhibition. Although its display right next to a series of missiles from the Hwasal family suggests that it is intended as an alternative launcher, the differences in the TEL and launch tube indicate a deviation in function that is not yet fully understood. One possibility is that the system in question is responsible for launching Hwasal variants with upscaled warheads, such as the Hwasal-1 Ra-3 tested in April of 2024.

Two Pulhwasal-3 SLCMs are launched from the Gorae-class during tests in early 2023. (KCBC)

A Pulhwasal-3 SLCM is launched during testing in early 2024. (KCBC)

The as yet unidentified and untested suspected GLCM during the 75th anniversary of the Workers' Party of Korea parade in 2020. Between being displayed at the Self-Defence-2021 exhibition and the National Defence Development-2024 exhibition, changes to the launch tubes were apparent. (KCBC)

The Hwasal-1 and Hwasal-2 (left) and the Pulhwasal-3 at the National Defence Development-2024 exhibition. At the top, the updated launcher for the as yet unidentified GLCM. (KCBC)

Given a light and particularly small nuclear weapon design, it is possible to mount nuclear warheads on a range of weaponry usually employing conventional explosives. These include, but are certainly not limited to, gravity bombs dropped by aircraft, large SAMs and AShMs, torpedoes and offensive and defensive mines. Such weapons facilitate far more effective tactical deployment of nuclear weapons than can be achieved through ballistic missiles alone, and greatly diversify the situations that may give rise to a nuclear exchange. Nuclear torpedoes might for instance be fitted to some of the DPRK's submarines for use against ROK/US Navy fleets when their destruction is absolutely vital to the war effort. In such a scenario, a single torpedo could easily decimate an entire carrier group when given the chance, which given the extensive anti-submarine activities during times of war, remains a relatively unlikely prospect however. Likewise, if a nuclear warhead were to be designed for large SAMs such as the S-200, aerial operations over the Korean Peninsula could essentially be countered en masse (sidelining the advances made in electronic countermeasures), once again assuming its operators are given the chance to fire it. Nuclear mines are less at risk of facing countermeasures, and the strategy of detonating preplaced nuclear mines in tactical positions on your own territory once a hostile force manages to breach the lines has been utilised by other nations in the past, including by the US in South Korea during the Cold War period.[98]

While most of these applications, especially on legacy armament, remain speculative in the case of the DPRK, unconfirmed reports by defectors dating back to 2009 claimed research on nuclear mines and torpedoes had already commenced, with the first nuclear torpedoes expected to be completed by 2012.[99] [100] One such programme was suddenly made known to the world in early 2023, when Kim Jong Un attended tests of the so-called Haeil ('tsunami') nuclear torpedo. Rather than consisting of an existing torpedo fitted with a nuclear warhead, it was revealed that this weapons system has more in common with the Russian Status-6 'Poseidon', which is a strategic system designed to flood coastal cities with its powerful multi-megaton warhead. Unlike the Status-6 however, the North Korean design evidently utilises conventional propulsion instead of a special nuclear reactor, and has a far more leisurely speed of just under eight knots (compared to up to 100 knots for the Status-6). It is believed that the designation Haeil refers to a family of nuclear torpedo designs however, and each type is liable to have different characteristics. The very first displayed, and also one of the largest, is believed to have a diameter of some 1.5 metres and a length of more than 10 metres, and is capable of cruising at a depth of 80 to 150 metres for at least 59 hours and 12 minutes, according to descriptions of its single publicised test. The commentary went on to state that development had begun in 2012, and that over 50 tests of the system had been conducted over the past two years, of which 29 attended by Kim Jong Un. Furthermore, it stated that:

> The mission of the underwater nuclear strategic weapon is to stealthily infiltrate into operational waters and make a super-scale radioactive tsunami through underwater explosion to destroy naval striker groups and major operational ports of the enemy.
>
> This nuclear underwater attack drone can be deployed at any coast and port or towed by a surface ship for operation.[101]

A second type apparently known as the Haeil-1 was tested just days later to a simulated distance of 600 kilometres, reportedly taking 41 hours and 27 minutes to reach its target.[102] Although it is impossible to estimate its size from the images provided, it might be that a schematic of a possible torpedo fitted with the Hwasan-31 tactical nuclear warhead depicts this design, in which case it has a diameter of approximately one metre. Yet another type was tested in May the same year, this time reportedly cruising 1,000 kilometres over the course of 71 hours and six minutes (consistent with the same speed of below eight knots). The livery of the torpedo in question discerned it from either type displayed before, and it was referred to as the Haeil-2 instead.[103] The 70th anniversary of 'Victory Day' in July 2023 added yet another type to the growing list of known variants, with four massive pump-jet powered torpedoes measuring some 16 metres in length and 1.5 metres in diameter driven through the capital on flat beds. Though there have been no known tests of this variant, it is possible that an object spotted on satellite imagery at Sinpho shipyard in 2020 concerned the same programme. If only to drive home the point that the Haeil torpedo family has been around for quite a while without anyone noticing, in early 2024 reports referred to the test of a Haeil-5-23 nuclear torpedo. Without any accompanying images or claims with regards to performance, all that may be gleaned from this event is that at least five types of nuclear torpedoes exist, and that not just the Hwasan-31 tactical nuclear warhead may be carried.[104] All types displayed are believed to be much too large to be fitted to conventional torpedo tubes, and will require dedicated vessels and launch facilities for their deployment. With North Korean news commentary suggesting deployment from unidentified surface vessels, this introduces yet another reason to consider even ostensibly civilian naval vessels as viable targets during times of conflict. While a 'radioactive tsunami' is unlikely to be triggered by a tactical nuclear warhead, the prospect of large amounts of nuclear torpedoes striking (military) ports in the region once more raises the bar for the detection and destruction of nuclear weapons delivery systems.

Left: Kim Jong Un at a showroom displaying the Haeil nuclear torpedo. It is unknown what the precise numbered designation of this type is, or indeed if it has one. (KCBC)

Below: A Haeil-2 nuclear torpedo during testing in early 2024. (KCBC)

A Haeil-1 nuclear torpedo during testing in early 2023. (KCBC)

An as yet unnamed variant of the Haeil family during the 70th anniversary of 'Victory Day' in July 2023. Note the pump-jet propulsion, and what could be an exhaust system for diesel propulsion. (KCBC)

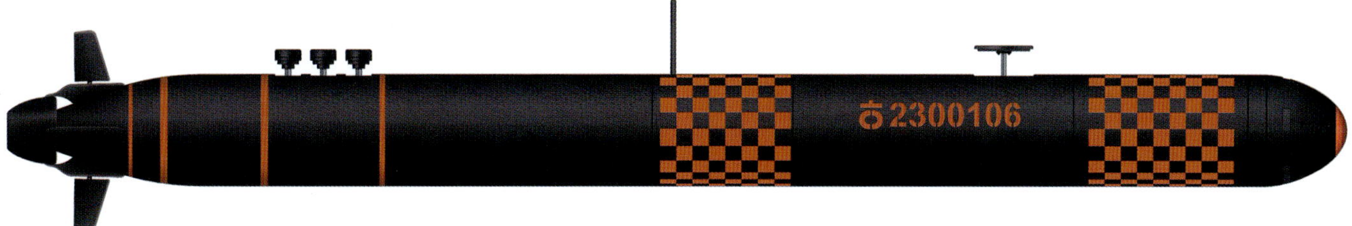

This as yet unnamed Haeil variant measures approximately 16 metres in length and 1.5 metres in diameter, bearing a striking resemblance to Russia's Status-6 'Poseidon' nuclear-powered unmanned underwater vehicle, but is approximately four metres shorter and not nuclear powered. Deploying this system from submarines would necessitate entirely new submarine designs, and North Korea might initially plan to deploy it from shore installations or retrofitted vessels, such as cargo ships. It is believed that the Status-6 can also be launched from specialised containers installed on the seabed, a launching method that has undoubtedly piqued North Korea's interest as well. (Artwork by Anderson Subtil)

National Aerospace Technology Administration

Concomitant to North Korea's ballistic missile industry is the National Aerospace Technology Administration,[105] tasked with developing space launch vehicles, satellites and associated technologies. Although the DPRK's space programme has often been proclaimed to be peaceful in nature, in the past it has often been accused of testing technologies that may be incorporated in ICBMs through it, and even of using its supposed SLVs as a crude nuclear deterrent. Since experimental engines, components and entire missile sections have indeed been used ever since the first official launch of a satellite in August 1998, there is little doubt that research results gained from the space programme may be used directly for ballistic missile development. Nevertheless, the prolific analyses of what payloads modified variants of North Korean SLVs may carry over specific distances served as little more than interesting speculation, and such use was never realistic. Given the fact that the DPRK has shown remarkably little hesitance in simply testing ballistic missile technologies overtly without any attempt at concealment, it may be concluded that the North Korean space programme indeed serves no large role in its offensive military capabilities.

Still, SLVs may be used to launch satellites that serve military purposes. The slowly improving reliability and markedly reduced reliance on imported parts witnessed during the latest satellite launch attempts show North Korea has ambitious plans in this regard – and its Kwangmyongsong-4 earth observation satellite launched in February 2016 could be construed as the first step towards a rudimentary spy satellite capability. And indeed, during the 8th Congress of the WPK in 2021 the goal of producing and launching a military reconnaissance satellite was first expressly stated, with 2022 seeing a rapid progression of tests purported to be working towards that aim. In December 2022, a test satellite was launched with an SLV that utilised a modified Hwasong-7 as its first stage and that carried a payload 'with one panchromatic camera for 20m resolution test, two multispectral cameras, video transmitter and transmitters and receivers of various bands, control devices and batteries'. Commentary to the test suggested launch preparations for the actual satellite were projected to be finished by April 2023, perhaps with the hopes of a launch prior to the birth date of Kim Il Sung on 15 April (like the Kwangmyongsong-3, which was launched on 13 April 2012). Instead, the first launch of the Chollima-1 SLV occurred on 31 May 2023. The three stage design, based on an amalgamation of ballistic missile components thought primarily to include the Hwasong-17's first stage engines, failed when the second stage ignited prematurely. A follow-up attempt on 23 August met a similar fate, this time failing during the third stage. A launch on 21 November finally succeeded in placing the so-called Malligyong-1 reconnaissance satellite in orbit, establishing for the first time a rudimentary North Korean spy satellite capability. While South Korea claimed that analysis of the debris from the first launch showed that it 'had no military use at all as a reconnaissance satellite', even a very basic independent earth observation capability would have obvious military use cases.[106] Moreover, it is clear that the North Korean programme is more than just a token effort, with the satellite even demonstrating an orbital manoeuvring ability by raising its perigee in 2024.[107] Besides preserving the one reconnaissance satellite it now has, North Korea on 27 May 2024 attempted to launch an improved reconnaissance satellite, which it called the Malligyong-1-1. Evidently dissatisfied with the performance of the Chollima-1, it claimed it had used a new type SLV with a 'liquid oxygen + petroleum engine'. While older SLV such as the ones based around the Hwasong-7's engines also used 'petroleum'-based (kerosene) fuels, the reference has led some to speculate that the system involved instead concerned a Russian Angara SLV. Whatever the case, the launch failed spectacularly shortly after take-off, and the satellite was once again lost.[108]

Aside from reconnaissance, military satellites may be useful to North Korea's (ballistic) missile programme by providing a much-needed alternative means of relaying telemetry. Its consideration of this use case is evident from Glocom's GS-2600-0660 'Ballistic Missile Telemetry System', which explicitly refers to a satellite data link as an option.[109] Other potential developments, such as a satellite-based early warning system designed to detect ballistic missile launches against the country, or even a manned space programme, will indubitably be in the DPRK's crosshairs. Nevertheless, the resources and technologies required for such projects are substantial – to any other nation sufficiently so to outweigh their potential benefit to the military or even just national pride.

A Paektusan-1 SLV on display. The description reads 'Chosun' on either stage, the first of which appears to consist of a modified Hwasong-7 and the second a modified Hwasong-6. (KCBC)

A Malligyong-1 reconnaissance satellite seen during a visit by Kim Jong Un in May 2023. (KCBC)

The Chollima-1 SLV during its first successful launch in November 2023. Note the large payload fairing. (KCBC)

Kim Jong Un is shown an Angara SLV at the Vostochny Cosmodrome during a visit to Russia in September 2023. There is some indication to suggest North Korea was looking to acquire SLV technologies in exchange for its military support during the Russo-Ukrainian War. Ironically, South Korea's KSLV-1 too is based on the Angara. (KCBC)

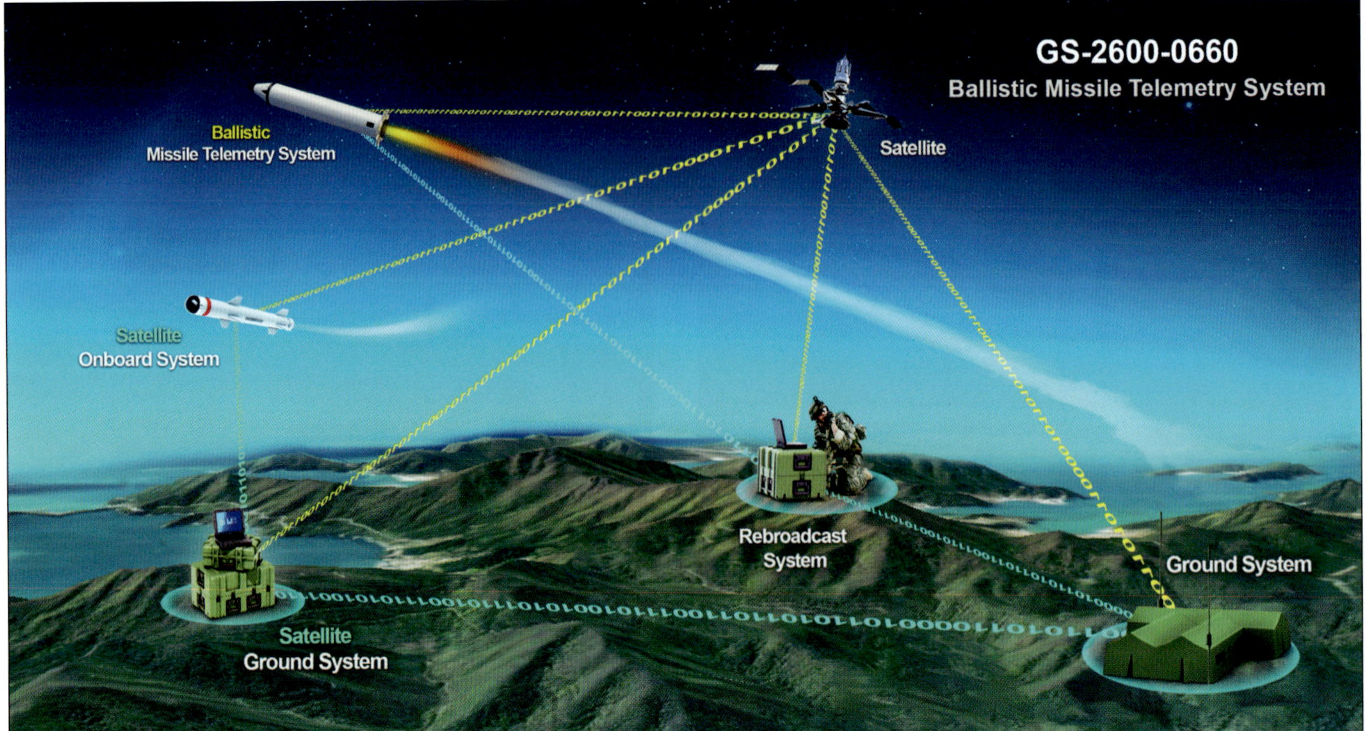

A schematic explaining Glocom's GS-2600-0660 'Ballistic Missile Telemetry System'. The ballistic missile shown is reminiscent of the Pukguksong-2. (Glocom)

Weapons of Mass Destruction

Despite the size, imposing looks and technological sophistication of the various delivery systems available to the MGB, in the end the real danger posed is contained within the actual warheads. Although ballistic missiles are capable of using conventional munitions, most commonly HE, cluster, or thermobaric warheads, they are also the deployment method par excellence for WMDs. The DPRK has invested in weapons of mass destruction in virtually every category of relevance, and its arsenal of WMDs is imposing as a result. Although nuclear weapons are by far the most feared and certainly the most widely promulgated type of WMDs, featuring in headlines since the conception of its nuclear weapons programme in the previous century, North Korea is in possession of far more types of strategic armament than just its nuclear missiles. Chemical, biological and radiological weaponry is either confirmed or in the latter case expected to be actively researched, developed and stockpiled, and a range of alternative delivery methods for nuclear weapons diversify the North's strategic capabilities. With this weaponry, it could afflict unprecedented casualties in its immediate region, and more importantly, potentially invoke a full-scale nuclear war.

A nose cone for the Hwasong-5 or -6 missile. Even for these comparatively small ballistic missiles the DPRK is believed to be able to produce sufficiently miniaturised warheads to be fitted, making them suitable for the delivery of all types of WMDs. (KCBC)

Any conflict to erupt on the Korean Peninsula is likely to eventually devolve into the use of WMDs, either from the onset of hostilities or after the North's main push has ground to a halt before meeting its desired objectives. As the use of WMDs dramatically transmogrifies the essence of warfare itself, conventional military wisdom will be insufficient to prepare for the unpredictable turns of fate such a war might bring. Although various types of WMDs have been used in armed strife of the past, infamously marking the end of the Second World War in the Pacific and, in the case of chemical weapons, causing widespread casualties in a multitude of conflicts, the type of strategic war the Korean Peninsula is liable to see will be unlike anything yet encountered both in intensity and types of weaponry deployed. While the possibility that both sides will be able to restrain themselves from using WMDs cannot be ruled out, it is deemed highly likely that North Korea intends to fully exploit the advantages gained from deploying chemical weaponry at the least. Peacetime efforts to diminish the threats posed by North Korean WMDs therefore remain relevant even if their chance of success is low. Ever since the DPRK's accession to, and subsequent withdrawal from, the Treaty on the Non-Proliferation of Nuclear Weapons (NPT) in 1985 such efforts have been at the forefront of North Korean international interaction, with the prospect of nuclear disarmament and a thaw in relations consistently followed by disintegration of talks and increased tensions. The latest iteration of this cycle unexpectedly initiated in early 2018 involved the historic first meeting of US president Donald Trump and North Korean leader Kim Jong Un, a hallmark of the unique unpredictability inherent to the Korea conundrum. Since its failure, no serious attempts have been mounted, and the North Korean nuclear state appears to be a permanent fact.

Nuclear Weapons

North Korean nuclear ambitions are thought to have originated even before the events of the 1980s, and its desires to conduct nuclear research, including operating a nuclear reactor, were noted as early as 1958.[110] During the 1960s, the Yongbyon Nuclear Scientific Research Centre was established to this end, operating an IRT-2000 research reactor delivered by the Soviet Union as a result of agreements on cooperation in atomic energy research in 1959.[111] Nevertheless, North Korean requests for closer cooperation and particularly the delivery of an actual nuclear power plant were denied, and the existing research reactor was continually upgraded to operate at larger power outputs and using higher enriched uranium instead.[112] [113] Only after a spate of visits by Kim Il Sung to the Soviets in the early 1980s did the construction of a new experimental reactor capable of creating large amounts of plutonium of use in a nuclear weapons programme commence. As relations warmed, the Soviet Union conceded assistance and by 1986 the reactor first went into operation. However, this assistance did not come without assurances to the Soviets, and it appears North Korean entry to the NPT was a prerequisite.[114] Although this marked the start of decades of fierce diplomatic conflict over the DPRK's nuclear programme, the first public indications that anything was amiss came only in 1992, when the International Atomic Energy Agency (IAEA) found discrepancies between the North's declared nuclear facilities, equipment and materials and what their analysis showed.[115] The North Korean nuclear dream had clearly originated much earlier however, with work on what would later become its Punggye-ri Nuclear Test Site initiated already in 1985 or 1986.[116] After the North Koreans (repeatedly) refused access to nuclear facilities in order to resolve the discrepancies related to its nuclear programme, the issue came to a head in March 1993, when the DPRK announced it would withdraw from the NPT.[117] Although following UN Security Council resolution 825 this was suspended a day before it was brought into effect, and nuclear talks commenced, in May 1994 the North Koreans began unloading fuel rods from the new reactor without supervision, a move which denied the IAEA the possibility of ever accurately determining the amount of nuclear material processed at the site.[118] The situation came close to open war when the US considered striking the North's nuclear facilities in 1994, which according to some would have surely prompted the KPA to invade the South in a conflict that was assessed to ultimately have the potential to cost the lives of over one million on both sides combined.[119]

In what at the time was heralded as a major diplomatic success, a deal known as the Agreed Framework was made, which would see North Korea remain in the NPT, shut down its existing nuclear reactors and cease the reprocessing of fuel rods. In exchange, the US would construct two large light water reactors, which are less easily used to produce weapons-grade plutonium, and ensure deliveries of heavy oil in order to compensate for the loss of energy production in the meantime. Support for the agreement, which was never drawn up as a binding treaty, faltered on the US side shortly after its signing, and late deliveries of the promised oil, indefinite delays on the power plants' construction and allegations that North Korea was running a covert uranium enrichment programme led to its breakdown in late 2002. By January 2003, North Korea announced its final withdrawal from the NPT, setting off an ineffective period of six-party talks, to which the DPRK, ROK, US, PRC, Japan and Russia were part, during which the North Korean nuclear programme produced its first tangible results.

Conducting its first (widely held to be only partially, or even not at all, successful) nuclear weapons test in October 2006, it followed up with another in 2009 after the six-party talks were discontinued. In the 2010s, the pace of nuclear weapon testing accelerated commensurately to the increased rate of missile tests during the same period, in an apparent manifestation of Kim Jong Un's Pyongjin Line policies. Evidence suggests the decade began with an unreported low-yield nuclear test in May 2010, although the event largely escaped public scrutiny at the time.[120] A third publicised test took place in 2013, and other than merely demonstrating a nuclear capability, the KCNA claim that the device involved was geared towards miniaturisation indicated ambitions of creating a reliable and workable offensive capability.[121] Another test followed in January 2016, claimed by the North's media broadcasts to have been of the country's first hydrogen bomb.[122] Given the test's unimpressive yield, this claim is generally considered to be false, but a boosted fission design (which uses nuclear fusion to boost the yield gained from fission) similar to the RDS-6, which the Soviet Union in turn claimed was its first hydrogen bomb, seems plausible.[123] Shortly after, Kim Jong Un was pictured on a visit to a missile factory outside Pyongyang, during which he observed a mock-up of a seemingly crude but compact nuclear weapon. Analyses of this design are not always in agreement about its precise characteristics, including if it indeed employs boosted fission, but the fact that it is small and light enough to be fitted to North Korean ballistic missiles is undeniable. A second test of a compact design in September 2017 supposedly explored this approach further, attaining a greater yield while being light enough for the warhead to be mounted on a missile, according to KCNA.[124] A year (and two successful ICBM tests) later, Kim Jong Un was again pictured inspecting a nuclear warhead design, clearly showcasing in the process that it was designed to allow deployment by the Hwasong-14. More importantly, the mock-up showcased was undeniably of a compact thermonuclear weapon, weighing perhaps between just 255 and 360 kilogrammes.[125] Immediately after, North Korea announced it had tested this design, generating shockwaves indicating a nuclear detonation with a yield in the low hundreds of kilotonnes of TNT, corresponding with KCNA claims that:

> The H-bomb, the explosive power of which is adjustable from tens kiloton to hundreds kiloton, is a multi-functional thermonuclear nuke with great destructive power which can be detonated even at high altitudes for super-powerful EMP attack according to strategic goals.[126]

Similar in outward appearance to the US W88 thermonuclear warhead, if the claimed capabilities of this design are accurate then they mean the North has gained the ability to deploy lightweight variable yield thermonuclear warheads. What is more, if it can indeed be used to exploit the high-altitude electromagnetic pulse effect, such a device could easily disrupt electronics in vast swaths of northeast Asia, paralysing unprepared militaries and profoundly damaging one of the most important economic regions in the world.

In early 2023, the DPRK's nuclear abilities had apparently evolved once more, with Kim Jong Un visiting a display where 10 supposed Hwasan-31 ('Volcano-31') tactical nuclear warheads and various delivery systems were presented. The Hwasan-31 has been miniaturised further from the 2017 design, and features a sturdy casing that obscures most of the device's external characteristics. As such, it is difficult to ascertain whether it concerns a fission-boosted weapon, and analysis of its dimensions only suggest an estimated weight of roughly 250 kilogrammes, and a diameter of the casing of some 500mm. Platforms confirmed to be compatible with the Hwasan-31 are the entire (modern) Hwasong-11 family, the 600mm super-large MRL, the Hwasal family, and at least one suspected nuclear torpedo. With various tests of these weapons simulating nuclear airbursts (which exploit blast wave physics to maximise the destructive effect) at differing altitudes of around 800 metres, the Hwasan-31 could well be a variable yield design in the tens of kilotonnes range. Curiously, statements made by Kim Yo Jong in October 2024 seemed to imply that North Korean MRLs (presumably the 600mm types) are capable of deploying a nuclear warhead equivalent to 900 tonnes of TNT.[127] If this refers to the Hwasan-31, it would be unusually light for a warhead of that size. References to a Haeil-5-23 nuclear torpedo seem to suggest that another nuclear warhead design, possibly designated the Hwasan-23, is in advanced stages of development. Unfortunately, no further information on this warhead is currently available.

It is impossible to definitively link the showcased designs with any of the tests conducted over the past years, and North Korea may in fact through them be attempting to deceive observers into thinking their nuclear programme is more advanced than it really is. However, the mock-ups, warhead designs and general advances made are plausible at this stage, and given the degree of transparency in other,

A relatively simple fission-based nuclear warhead mock-up showcased in March 2016. The Hwasong-13 variant in the back had at this point presumably been foregone, and as images exist of Kim Jong Il inspecting a similar device prior to 2011 this mock-up may not have represented the most advanced technology available at the time. (KCBC)

A far more advanced, possibly variable yield thermonuclear warhead mock-up showcased just prior to a nuclear weapons test of what was claimed to be the same design in September 2017. (KCBC)

Kim Jong Un inspects a (presumably inert) Hwasan-31 tactical nuclear warhead in March 2023. The poster details eight different weapons systems supposedly capable of deploying this warhead. A total of 10 Hwasan-31s were on display here. (KCBC)

more verifiable, aspects of the development of the DPRK's nuclear deterrence in the past years, the North Korean claims may justifiably be taken at face value. The development of nuclear weapons and their ballistic delivery systems was coupled with that of what appears to be genuine heat shields, nose cone fairings and re-entry vehicles, all but conclusively proving that North Korea is now in possession of at least a functional regional nuclear deterrent. Since its warhead mock-ups were light and small enough to be mounted on virtually all of its ballistic missile designs, the range of platforms that may be used to deliver a nuclear payload is broad and nigh impossible to pre-emptively destroy. Its uranium enrichment programme is estimated to be sufficient to produce material for fissile-based nuclear weapons at a relatively high pace, with approximately 50 (but potentially up to 90) currently thought to be in their arsenal as of 2024.[128] It should be noted however that this number is subject to a large degree of uncertainty due to a lack of on-site inspections and technical data on North Korean enrichment facilities. Moreover, such facilities have been steadily expanded over the course of the past decades, with a September 2024 report of a visit by Kim Jong Un to the Kangson uranium enrichment plant quoting him as stating:

> We should not be complacent about the achievements we have made so far, but increase the number of centrifuges further and further enhance the individual separation ability of centrifuges, and push forward the project of introducing new-type centrifuges that have already reached the completion stage as planned, thereby further strengthening the foundation for the production of weapons-grade nuclear materials.[129]

While that visit as well as another in January 2025 to Yongbyon's uranium enrichment facilities provided a long-awaited look at the number and dimensions of modern North Korean centrifuges, estimates of the total production capacity remain fraught with uncertainties not least because the underlying technology of the centrifuges themselves remains uncertain. Some have suggested the cooling coils installed since the last inspection in 2010 may indicate a switch to carbon fibre composite rotors, which would increase performance and mirror developments in Iranian uranium enrichment facilities.[130] Another suspected new enrichment facility was identified at Yongbyon in June 2025, suggesting North Korea's nuclear arsenal will continue to grow at an increasing rate.[131]

A heat shield is subjected to an exhaust flame from a rocket engine. (KCBC)

Kim Jong Un tours the uranium enrichment facility at Kangson in September 2024, providing the first clear photographs of North Korean Zippe-type centrifuges. (KCBC)

Kim Jong Un inspects Zippe-type centrifuges of the same manufacture at Yongbyon in January 2025. Note the extensive network of piping coming from the centrifuges, a recent addition suspected to be for cooling purposes. (KCBC)

To the DPRK, such an arsenal is sufficient to ensure a strategic first strike ability at least against its immediate environment (i.e. South Korea, Japan, and possibly Guam), while a second strike ability is rapidly materialising.[132] While a 2013 ordinance stipulating the North's nuclear weapons policies ruled out use unless to 'repel invasion or attack from a hostile nuclear weapons state and make retaliatory strikes', an update to the law promulgated in 2022 was substantially more lax.[133] For instance, it included the following as an acceptable condition: 'In case the need for operation for preventing the expansion and protraction of a war and taking the initiative in the war in contingency is inevitably raised'.[134] Even if the majority of its ballistic missiles carrying nuclear warheads are destroyed prior to launch, intercepted or otherwise countered, just a single detonation in the 100–200 kilotonnes of TNT range on a major population centre could inflict millions of casualties in an instant.[135] This is likely to be held at least temporarily sufficient as a nuclear deterrent, which means the DPRK has begun to fully divert efforts towards the mass production of tactical nuclear weapons. Such weapons are reportedly managed by the Haekpangasoe ('Nuclear Trigger') national combined nuclear weapons management system. This system was seemingly developed in the early 2020s, with progressive tests aimed at simulating a nuclear counterstrike involving a variety of nuclear weapons delivery systems performed since early 2023.

Wider applicability of tactical nuclear weapons increases the chance of a tactical nuclear exchange, which in practice would soon result in a strategic nuclear exchange. The fact that these weapons, certainly when deployed by ballistic missiles, are now available means the moment the tide turns against the KPA in a conflict, it is highly likely to resort to the use of nuclear weapons. This would then be answered in kind in an attempt to neutralise all of the North Korean military and particularly its nuclear assets, thus provoking a strategic nuclear war. In a different scenario, the DPRK may even declare North Korean soil to be off-limits to foreign militaries on penalty of a strategic nuclear strike, and thus resort to the use of strategic weaponry straight away when its territories are threatened. This is the only even remotely, with the emphasis on remotely, plausible scenario in which the DPRK might end up victorious in a new Korean conflict: effectively holding conquered areas hostage at the threat of launching a nuclear strike against the region. Whatever the case, the US response to the use of nuclear weapons is likely to be both decisive and devastating, typically consisting of a strike by one of its Ohio-class sub-surface ballistic nuclear submarines (SSBNs) which alone would be sufficient, and comfortably so, to destroy most of the North's cities and military strongholds. While North Korea's short-to-medium range missile arsenal has grown sizeable and advanced enough to remove any doubt of its ability to inflict massive damage on its neighbours, many of its long-ranged nuclear delivery methods as yet require some time to prepare before launch. This fact, combined with systems like Ground-Based Midcourse Defence, might mean casualties in the USA remain relatively limited. If the North Koreans were hell-bent on achieving a more potent nuclear arsenal, they could also develop radiological nuclear weapons, designed to maximise their radiation output and thus render large swaths of land uninhabitable when detonated. The development of such weaponry is considered highly immoral, yet doing so in secrecy would negate the advantages posed to the perceived strength of the DPRK's nuclear deterrence, meaning there is usually little point in going down this route.

More probable avenues of development for the future include the aforementioned diversification of the nuclear arsenal, in both the tactical and larger strategic direction, as well as the widespread introduction of newer, more advanced weaponry with such characteristics as variable yield and high-altitude detonation capabilities. Another technology frequently alluded to in press statements is that of the MIRV, which sees multiple warheads mounted to a single missile in order to maximise effect, decrease chances of interception and even destroy various targets in one go. Such capabilities were first tested in June 2024, with a modified Hwasong-17 missile with a solid-fuelled second stage lofting three separate warheads as well as a decoy according to state media. The warheads were then reportedly guided towards three targets at ranges between 170 to 200 kilometres, although Seoul's Joint Chiefs of Staff claimed instead that the missile had suffered a failure and blown up.[136] Further research in the area of MaRVs, decoys and quasi-ballistic missiles similarly aids ballistic missile warheads in their safe descent, all adding to the credibility of the DPRK's nuclear deterrence. On the ground, this is achieved by diversifying platforms which can carry nuclear weapons; introducing nuclear missile silos, SSB(N)s and other dedicated platforms.

Biological and Chemical Weaponry

In discussions of the DPRK's WMD arsenal, nuclear weapons tend to be the focus, if not the sole point of attention. Although this has its justifications, especially given the rapid advancements in this field of the past decades, the other main types of WMDs have been extensively researched and invested in by North Korea as well, and pose a different if not equally grave threat to its opponents. Notably, the use of chemical and even biological weaponry is thought to be inherent to the KPA's conventional warfare doctrine, meaning that their effect on battlefield conditions will have to be taken into consideration to properly analyse any potential combat situation. North Korea is not a signatory of the Chemical Weapons Convention (CWC), prohibiting the production stockpiling and use of chemical weapons. Nevertheless, it has acceded to the Biological Weapons Convention (BWC) and the Geneva Protocol, the latter with the stipulation that it ceases to be binding against other parties that do not observe the prohibitions of the protocol. Although this forbids the first use of chemical and biological weapons, and in the latter case even development, production and stockpiling, it is unlikely the DPRK will feel much pressure to adhere to these treaties during wartime. Just one indication of a willingness to utilise this category of WMDs was demonstrated by the assassination of Kim Jong Un's half-brother Kim Jong Nam in February 2017 by use of a binary VX nerve agent on foreign soil. Of course, such treaties as the Geneva Protocol have been liberally ignored by certain parties in conflicts of the past, notably the Iran-Iraq War and more recently the Syrian Civil War. In modern times, treaties like the CWC and BWC have resulted in many nations taking steps to either reduce or fully eliminate their declared chemical and biological weapons stocks, preventing their use in any conflict. To the DPRK, this actually presents an unusual advantage: since its adversaries have destroyed their chemical and biological stockpiles (with the USA destroying its final munition in late 2023), it would be able to use such weaponry itself without fear of a proportional response.[137]

Its biological weapon stockpiles, though potentially highly deadly, are also the most disputed. Its biological weapons programme has been reported on by several sources over the past decades, but its true extent and the degree to which these weapons are produced, stockpiled and deployed is a matter of controversy. Highly telling however, is the fact that defected North Korean soldiers were found to have been vaccinated against biological agents such as smallpox.[138] This suggests that the DPRK intends to use biological weaponry in a future conflict, given that no other parties would be liable to use it, and has prepared its military to deal with this eventuality. Conversely, neither the South Korean population nor the military has been vaccinated against mainstream biological agents such as smallpox or anthrax.[139] Whatever scope biological weapon use might see during a conflict, current evidence points towards significant North Korean interest in this field, with an extensive infrastructure in place to facilitate research and production of biological weaponry. Interestingly, the first accusations about biological weapons on the Korean Peninsula were not made against the DPRK, but rather made by the DPRK, China and the Soviet Union alleging that the USA was conducting biological warfare in the course of the Korean War. These allegations have now largely been debunked as defamation efforts set up mainly by China and the DPRK and in order to explain the outbreaks of typhus, typhoid and smallpox among the Korean population. Still, North Korean interest in the possible use of such diseases as weapons must have been sparked early on, and the importation of pathogens and equipment for study from abroad supposedly commenced after Kim Il Sung ordered the 'concentrated development of biological weapons' in 1961, stating that biological warfare would be 'most effective in war in the future'.[140] Production of agents suitable for biological warfare is reported to have commenced in the 1980s, with 13 different types said to have been in production by 1992.[141] In modern times, the ROK MoD estimates that at least three production facilities and seven research centres exist, with 14 agents in its possession.[142] [143] [144] Many of these, specifically anthrax, botulism, plague, smallpox and tularemia, are classified as Category A biological weapons, which have a high potential for dissemination and high mortality rates.

Merely the possession of pathogens does not imply an ability to successfully deploy them or even produce them at large enough scales for their effective use. For comparison, the Soviet Union's biological weapons programme 'yielded only 13 weaponizable agents despite an investment of 40,000 personnel over 63 years (from 1928 to 1991)'.[145] Modern advancements and a better understanding of pathogens in the modern era might have yielded significant advances in this area, yet the useful weaponisation of biological weapons remains a very difficult task. It is likely the DPRK has focussed on weaponising some of the agents that are easiest to produce, store and deploy, amongst which are anthrax and smallpox. These are on their own sufficient to cause mass casualties in dense cities such as Seoul, and require extensive biological reconnaissance, clean-up, vaccination and quarantine protocols from the opposing side once deployed, severely disrupting military operations and society as a whole. Successful outbreaks of such diseases in a large city such as Seoul could result in millions of casualties, for instance through the contamination of water supplies. However, the first aim of their use on the Korean Peninsula will be to complicate military operations. In this role, aerosolised biological agents could be released through iron bombs or artillery against military bases, ports and air bases, which would essentially be taken out of operation until, and perhaps even after, a lengthy clean-up. Coverage of a July 2017 visit by Kim Jong Un to the Pyongyang Bio-technical Institute showed equipment and materials that could be used to produce large batches of military-grade anthrax. Although the facility, which was built in the early 2010s, was claimed to be involved in the production of bio-pesticides, the technology is considered dual-use and could be swiftly converted to military ends, thus indicating an advanced anthrax production capability indeed exists in the DPRK.[146]

Given the threat posed by biological weapons, it would seem self-evident that the ROK has an extensive system in place to deal with such eventualities. However, unlike the USFK, the ROKA is not vaccinated against anthrax and smallpox.[147] Stockpiles of vaccinations for smallpox are insufficient to immunise even half the South Korean population, and an appropriate anthrax vaccine is awaiting approval before it can be handed to the military.[148] The US Department of Defense on the contrary has vaccinated all of its uniformed personnel present in the country for 15 consecutive days or longer against smallpox and anthrax since 2014, and together with the ROKA it has conducted nuclear, biological, chemical (NBC) warfare defence exercises since 2011.[149] These have since been continually extended in scope, and programmes for the introduction of new bio-surveillance equipment confirms both parties identify the threat as genuine. Despite the tactical advantages it may gain through them, biological attacks would likely elicit widespread condemnation from virtually the entire world community, and quite possibly lead to invasion by traditional allies of the DPRK. Still, there are plenty of scenarios in which these risks would be negated, irrelevant or simply considered acceptable. Given the right circumstances, a mere denial may be sufficient to stymie a response from the relevant powers, as was the case when chemical warfare was employed in the Iraq-Iran War and the Syrian Civil War. As such, the opening stages of a conflict on the Korean Peninsula may or may not see the use of biological warfare; yet by the time it concludes such use is deemed highly likely.

More is known about North Korea's chemical weapon programme, which, despite the fact that the DPRK continues to deny its existence, is believed to have commenced during the 1960s.[150] In the next decades, it proceeded to develop from a modest defensive capability into a large indigenous industry geared towards offensive operations by the 1990s.[151] In the meantime, it acquired samples of various chemical agents and the technology to produce them in small amounts.[152] By the end of the 1990s, it was estimated that stockpiles amounted to around 5,000 tonnes, with some eight production facilities capable of outputting the same every year.[153] Since then, there is no indication that this arsenal has been expanded or the production capacity enlarged, but the types of weaponry and associated equipment have continued to undergo improvement.[154] While those agents available in the previous century were judged to be used in weapon designs of the first and second generation (i.e. unitary warheads containing choking, blister, blood or nerve agents), nowadays the DPRK is thought to have increasing numbers of binary weapons containing nerve agents.[155] Although unitary warheads, which simply contain the chemical agent in a compressed form, are more effective on the battlefield, the chemicals they contain are typically unstable and will rapidly degrade while in storage, aside from being dangerous to work with. This means stocks need to be replaced often, with old weaponry requiring delicate dismantling efforts, or they will lose their potency, putting a strain on chemical weapons logistics. Binary chemical weapons, on the other hand, contain two precursors which combine in mid-flight to synthesise the desired chemical agent. This gives them much longer shelf-lives and makes them safer to handle, thus allowing for a wide deployment of large amounts of chemical weaponry even to ordinary combat units. While nerve agents are more acutely effective on the battlefield, choking, blister and blood agents may serve to encumber clean-up and countermeasures as they can affect through skin or gas masks and thus necessitate more extensive full-body protection. Furthermore, using a variety of different chemical agents on one front makes their successful identification and neutralisation more difficult.

Nevertheless, nerve agents will nowadays likely make up the bulk of the North Korean chemical stockpiles, and therefore differ for instance from Syria and Iraq's former chemical stockpiles in size, potency and usability. Furthermore, whereas the Middle Eastern theatres that saw chemical weapon use were often sparsely populated (of course, not due to the offending parties' best intentions), the prospective battlefields on the Southern end of the DMZ are typically densely urban. Some of the most potent chemical agents known to be in production in the DPRK are of the V-series of nerve agents, of which VX is the most well known and lethal. These agents differ from other, G-series, nerve agents in their persistence after use: whereas G-series agents may easily be cleansed off or degrade over time, those of the V-series remain toxic for long periods of time. The availability of VX to North Korea was notoriously showcased during the assassination of Kim Jong Nam in February 2017, which most likely saw the use of a binary variant of the deadly chemical. As Kim Jong Un's older half-brother in exile, Kim Jong Nam would have been eligible for leadership should some foreign power wish to depose him, and was therefore most likely deemed a threat to the regime in place. Two women that appeared to be under the impression they were participating in prank videos approached Kim Jong Nam at Kuala Lumpur International Airport, the one splashing a liquid in his face and the other covering it with a wet handkerchief. These two liquids were likely precursors for VX, and led to his death shortly thereafter. Extensive use of binary VX is very likely over the course of a large-scale conflict and would lead to massive casualties and widespread chaos on the receiving end.

Merely the availability of chemical armament is not sufficient to fully exploit the advantages of chemical warfare however, and the DPRK has also invested heavily in NBC protection gear, detection equipment and treatment methods. NBC defence units were established shortly after the Korean War, and are nowadays organic to most regiments in the KPA.[156] From the onset equipped with Soviet equipment including BTR-40Kh chemical reconnaissance vehicles, North Korea nowadays produces its own equivalents. In the case of NBC reconnaissance vehicles, these are based on jeeps and motorcycles with sidecars; examples of such vehicles have even been exported to Mozambique in a 2013 deal which included other chemical warfare detection and protection equipment.[157] Additionally, in keeping with Soviet design practices most North Korean fighting vehicles nowadays come with extensive NBC protection systems built in, allowing them to operate in contaminated areas without extended additional preparation. The widespread distribution of hazmat suits, gas masks and identification equipment alongside the deployment of such vehicles enables operations in areas that have been contaminated, thus giving a substantial military advantage over an unprepared foe.

The substantial industries, technological know-how and materials available as a result of the DPRK's WMD programmes also pose a significant proliferation risk. The most infamous example of a manifestation of this risk was tied to Syria's al-Kibar nuclear site, which was reportedly set up with extensive support from North Korea in the early to mid-2000s.[158] Thought to have been a nuclear reactor capable of processing reactor-grade uranium into weapons-grade plutonium, the facility was erected with secrecy as one of its most important design aspects. Nevertheless, Israeli air strikes completely destroyed the site in September 2007 before it could be completed, with a subsequent IAEA inspection confirming that it had most likely indeed harboured an undeclared nuclear reactor.[159] Continued cooperation on Syria's chemical weapons programme has also been reported, detailing deliveries of materials that could be used to produce chemical weapons and North Korean technicians working at chemical weapons and missile facilities even after Syria's accession to the CWC in 2013.[160] These instances clearly demonstrate a willingness to aid in the proliferation of even the most delicate military technologies, and show that this risk is anything but dormant in today's world.

Above: KPA soldiers using old chemical protection gear, including what appears to be the Second World War Soviet ShM-41 gas mask. (KCBC)

Right: Nowadays a derivative of the more modern PMK family is widely in use, and even exported to countries such as Syria. (KCBC)

Light vehicles such as these BTR-40Khs on parade are used for chemical reconnaissance. Note the yellow flags for demarcating contaminated areas. (KCBC)

CONCLUDING REMARKS

Time passes differently in the Korean Peninsula's northern half. Its intermittently starving population soldiers on through three generations of Kim family rule with little to show for it but a showcase capital and the tenuous survival of the rest of the nation, as any prospect of universal prosperity is carefully snuffed out. The country appears in stasis, paralysed by the stifling autocracy. Yet looking in from the outside, the situation has something akin to baking a pie. Events follow each other often at glacial speeds, and the careless observer is tempted to direct his or her attention elsewhere. Glancing back after what seems like just a moment, the pie is badly burnt, and the kitchen is about to burst into flames. The past decades have seen the DPRK go through an apparently endless cycle of provocations, weapons tests and resumptions of diplomatic actions, ultimately only to arrive back to the status quo. That status quo, unfortunately, is an illusion however. In the meantime, North Korea has seen the chance to acquire technologies Kim Jong Un's forefathers could not have dreamed to possess, and the nuclear genie is now fully out of the bottle. This coincides with not only the failure of any diplomatic effort (insofar as it ever stood a chance), but also with the emergence of substantial cracks in the UN's formerly unified stance regarding the isolated nation. For decades North Korea's efforts to proliferate sensitive weapons systems had been successfully mitigated, until post 2023 Russia's warming ties to the nation saw the transfer not only of massive amounts of artillery munitions, but also of ballistic missiles and even large deployments of North Korean special operations forces. Openly backed once more by at least one powerful foreign state, there is no telling what the next decade will bring to this forlorn corner of the world. When our gaze is next directed at the DPRK, will it be because the fire has ignited? How much might the flames eventually engulf?

Kim Jong Un and Russian president Vladimir Putin shake hands prior to a visit to the Vostochny Cosmodrome in September 2023. (Open source)

BIBLIOGRAPHY

Bermudez Jr., Joseph S. *Shield of the Great Leader: The Armed Forces of North Korea* (St Leonards: Allen & Unwin, 2001)

Carrel-Billiard, François, and Christine Wing, *Nuclear Energy, Nonproliferation, and Disarmament: Briefing Notes for the 2010 NPT Review Conference* (New York City: International Peace Institute, 2010)

Federal Research Division. *North Korea a country study* (Washington, DC.: Federal Research Division, 2008)

Gerardi, Greg J., and James A. Plotts. *An Annotated Chronology of DPRK Missile Trade and Developments* (Monterey: Nonproliferation Studies at the Monterey Institute of International Studies, 1994)

James Martin Center for Nonproliferation Studies at the Monterey Institute of International Studies *North Korea Biological Chronology* (Washington, DC.: Nuclear Threat Initiative, 2011)

James Martin Center for Nonproliferation Studies at the Monterey Institute of International Studies *North Korea Chemical Chronology* (Washington, DC.: Nuclear Threat Initiative, 2011)

James Martin Center for Nonproliferation Studies at the Monterey Institute of International Studies *North Korea Missile Chronology* (Washington, DC.: Nuclear Threat Initiative, 2012)

Kim Il-Sung. *The present situation and the tasks of our party; report at the conference of the Workers' Party of Korea* (Pyongyang: Foreign Languages Pub, 1966)

Korean Overseas Information Service. *Undermining Peace: North Korea's Infiltration Tunnels* (Seoul: Korean Overseas Information Service, 1991)

Marine Corps Intelligence Activity. *North Korea Country Handbook* (Quantico: Marine Corps Intelligence Activity, 1997)

Ministry of National Defence of the Republic of Korea. *Defense White Papers 2006-2022* (Yongsan, Seoul: Ministry of National Defence of the Republic of Korea, 2006-2022)

Schmucker, Robert, et al. *Raketenbedrohung 2.0: Technische und politische Grundlagen* (Hamburg: Mittler Verlag, 2015)

Singlaub, John K, et al. *Hazardous Duty* (New York City: Touchstone, 1992)

Zaloga, Steven J. *Scud Ballistic Missile and Launch Systems 1955–2005* (Oxford: Osprey, 2006)

ENDNOTES

Preface

1 We forsook the opportunity to use KPAAAAF.
2 Artworks in this book series serve mainly to elucidate subjects of which appropriate imagery is lacking, and as such certain volumes contain noticeably larger numbers of artworks than others.

Chapter 1

1 Republic of Korea Ministry of National Defense. 'Defense White Papers 2006-2022' *ROK MoD* http://www.mnd.go.kr/mbshome/mbs/mndEN/
2 Of course, the Special Operations Force has operated as a distinct branch for much of the Cold War as well, yet its formal separation as one of the five current KPA branches occurred only in the early 2010s.
3 Republic of Korea Ministry of National Defense. 'Defense White Papers 2006-2022' *ROK MoD*
4 Korean Overseas Information Service. Undermining Peace: North Korea's Infiltration Tunnels. (Seoul: Korean Overseas Information Service, 1991)
5 John K. Singlaub, et al. *Hazardous Duty*. (New York City, Touchstone, 1992)
6 Korean Overseas Information Service. 'Undermining Peace: North Korea's Infiltration Tunnels'
7 Korean Overseas Information Service. 'Undermining Peace: North Korea's Infiltration Tunnels'
8 Korean Overseas Information Service. 'Undermining Peace: North Korea's Infiltration Tunnels'
9 Korean Overseas Information Service. 'Undermining Peace: North Korea's Infiltration Tunnels'
10 This referred to the Korean Wall, a lengthy anti-tank fortification stretching along the Southern side of the MDL built in the late 1970s which frequently featured in North Korean propaganda in this period.
11 Central Intelligence Agency. 'The Korean Military Balance And Prospects For Hostilities On The Peninsula' *CIA FOIA* https://www.cia.gov/readingroom/document/0005569324
12 In reality, after a fierce month-long battle United Nations forces finally managed to dislodge North Korean and Chinese forces, at the cost of steep losses for either side.
13 Airborne insertion implies the use of parachutes to drop infantry over a target area, whereas airmobile operations involve roping down from helicopters or simply landing and offloading them on site.
14 Republic of Korea Ministry of National Defense. 'Defense White Papers 2006-2022' ROK MoD
15 유성운. '[천안함 폭침 1년]"北 특수부대원들 지금도 땅굴로 남한 침투"' (2011) *The Dong-a Ilbo* http://news.donga.com/Politics/3/00/20110323/35801211/1
16 This single escapee was not included in initial reports, but later comments by Kim Shin Jo, the only other survivor, indicate that the person in question is in fact current KPA general Pak Jae Gyong.
17 But not before the North Koreans attempted to convince them of the validity of the communist cause, leaving them with a warning not to contact the police. Had they instead elected to kill them, their planned mission might well have been a success.
18 Bemil Chosun. '2015년 서부전선 포격 사건 때 북한 특수부대가 복제한 K2 소총을 들고 있었다는 부사관의 증언' (2018) *bemil. chosun* http://bemil.chosun.com/nbrd/bbs/view.html?b_bbs_id=10044&num=214033
19 Josh Campbell. 'FBI arrests man allegedly helping prepare 'surprise attack' on South Korea' (2024) *CNN* https://edition.cnn.com/2024/12/03/us/fbi-arrests-man-allegedly-helping-prepare-surprise-attack-on-south-korea/index.html
20 Jae-Hong Kwon and Choi Yul-Mi. '육군 모 부대 해안 초소, 소령 사칭 총기 탈취사건 발생[이호인]' (1997) *MBC News* http://imnews.imbc.com/20dbnews/history/1997/1974254_19482.html
21 Additionally, he spent a good 20 minutes drinking tea and giving a motivational speech to the soldiers present.
22 The RGB may field another reconnaissance battalion that is to infiltrate and conduct operations in Japan or Guam during wartime.
23 Jacob Bogle. 'Military Operations in Urban Terrain: Redux' (2025) *AccessDPRK* https://mynorthkorea.blogspot.com/2025/02/military-operations-in-urban-terrain.html
24 Jacob Bogle. 'Where Did They Come From, Where Did They Go?' (2024) *AccessDPRK* http://mynorthkorea.blogspot.com/2024/12/where-did-they-come-from-where-did-they.html
25 Jane Lytvynenko. 'Inside an Elite Ukrainian Unit's Mission to Capture a North Korean Soldier' (2025) *The Wall Street Journal* https://www.wsj.com/world/inside-an-elite-ukrainian-units-mission-to-capture-a-north-korean-soldier-9d5f2ae6
26 Yi Wonju. 'Around 300 N.K. soldiers killed, 2,700 wounded during fight against Ukraine: S. Korea's spy agency' (2025) *Yonhap News Agency* https://en.yna.co.kr/view/AEN20250113005700315
27 Lee Minji. 'N. Korea presumed to send at least 3,000 more troops to Russia: JCS' (2025) *Yonhap News Agency* https://en.yna.co.kr/view/AEN20250327002251315
28 Koh Ewe. 'N Korea to send thousands to help rebuild Russia's Kursk' (2025) *BBC News* https://www.bbc.com/news/articles/cev0jrgx17ro
29 Munhwa Broadcasting Corporation. '체포된 북한 스파이 소지 러시아제 기관총,특수무기[박영민]' (1995) *MBC News* https://imnews.imbc.com/replay/1995/nwdesk/article/1964742_30705.html
30 KCNA. 'Respected Comrade Kim Jong Un Visits Special Operation Training Base under General Staff of KPA and Learns about Training of Soldiers' (2025) *KCNA Watch* https://kcnawatch.org/newstream/1756338088-665946622/Respected-Comrade-Kim-Jong-Un-Visits-Special-Operation-Training-Base-under-General-Staff-of-KPA-and-Learns-about-Training-of-Soldiers/
31 Lindsay Whitehurst. 'Man accused in night vision goggles case agrees to plea deal' (2015) *AP News* https://apnews.com/af1cfe6fd97e42248fe4f0b24a5bf27f/man-accused-night-vision-goggles-case-agrees-plea-deal
32 Tim Lister. 'North Korea's military aging but sizeable' (2010) *CNN* https://articles.cnn.com/2010-11-24/world/north.korea.capability_1_military-cooperation-massive-military-parade-pyongyang
33 Mads Brügger. '*The Mole: Undercover in North Korea*' (2020) *Wingman Media*
34 Byul Ahn. 'North Korean special forces train infiltration with paragliders... exercise surprise takeover of US, South Korean allies' (2017) *The Chosun Ilbo* https://www.chosun.com/site/data/html_dir/2017/10/10/2017101001091.html
35 Shin Joo Hyun. 'North Korean Submarine Helmsman Breaks 14-Year Silence' (2010) *Daily NK* https://www.dailynk.com/english/north-korean-submarine-helmsman-br/
36 A hefty reward system for tips leading to the arrest or killing of a North Korean operative is also sure to have contributed to the failure of the operation.
37 North Korea Leadership Watch. 'Guard Command' (2012) *North Korea Leadership Watch* http://www.nkleadershipwatch.org/guard-command-2/
38 Dave Philipps and Matthew Cole. 'How a Top Secret SEAL Team 6 Mission Into North Korea Fell Apart' (2025) *The New York Times* https://www.nytimes.com/2025/09/05/us/navy-seal-north-korea-trump-2019.html

Chapter 2

1 Korean Central News Agency. 'Day of Strategic Force Instituted in DPRK' (2016) *KCNA* www.kcna.co.jp/item//2016/201606/news25/20160625-32ee.html
2 Information obtained from the KPA Exhibition of Arms and Equipment in Pyongyang.

3 Information obtained from the KPA Exhibition of Arms and Equipment in Pyongyang.
4 Nuclear Threat Initiative. 'North Korean Missile Chronology' (2012) *Nuclear Threat Initiative* https://www.nti.org/media/pdfs/north_korea_missile_2.pdf?_=1327534760?_=1327534760
5 James Martin Center for Nonproliferation Studies. 'Chronology of North Korea's Missile Trade and Developments: 1960-1979' (2008) *James Martin Center for Nonproliferation Studies* https://www.nonproliferation.org/chronology-of-north-koreas-missile-trade-and-developments-1960-1979/
6 James Martin Center for Nonproliferation Studies. 'Chronology of North Korea's Missile Trade and Developments: 1960-1979' (2008) *James Martin Center for Nonproliferation Studies* https://www.nonproliferation.org/chronology-of-north-koreas-missile-trade-and-developments-1960-1979/
7 Which expressed itself in North Korean pilots flying Egyptian MiG-21s during the 1973 Yom Kippur War, as well as a number of state visits by president Hosni Mubarak to Pyongyang during the 1980s and 1990s.
8 Daniel A. Pinkston. 'CNS Special Report on North Korean Ballistic Missile Capabilities' (2006) *James Martin Center for Nonproliferation Studies* http://nautilus.org/wp-content/uploads/2011/12/0623.pdf
9 Information obtained from the KPA Exhibition of Arms and Equipment in Pyongyang.
10 Oryx Blog. 'Inconvenient Arms: North Korean Weapons In The Middle East' (2020) Oryx https://www.oryxspioenkop.com/2020/11/inconvenient-arms-north-korean-weapons.html
11 Daniel A. Pinkston. 'Interview with North Korean defector by CNS senior research associate Daniel A. Pinkston, November 1, 2000, Seoul' via https://www.nti.org/analysis/articles/north-korea-missile-capabilities/
12 The 'first' test of a missile in North Korean sources seems to refer to a first successful test of a finalised system, and as a result experimental tests are often reported prior to this date by Western sources.
13 Robert Schmucker et al. *Raketenbedrohung 2.0: Technische und politische Grundlagen* (Hamburg: Mittler Verlag, 2015)
14 Information obtained from the KPA Exhibition of Arms and Equipment in Pyongyang.
15 Information obtained from the KPA Exhibition of Arms and Equipment in Pyongyang.
16 Mads Brügger. *The Mole: Undercover in North Korea* (2020) Wingman Media
17 James Pearson and Hyonhee Shin. 'How a homemade tool helped North Korea's missile program' (2017) *Reuters* https://www.reuters.com/article/us-northkorea-missiles-technology/how-a-homemade-tool-helped-north-koreas-missile-program-idUSKBN1CH1I4
18 Steven J Zaloga. *Scud Ballistic Missile and Launch Systems 1955–2005* (Oxford: Osprey, 2006).
19 Korean Central News Agency. 'Kim Jong Un Guides Ballistic Rocket Test-Fire through Precision Control Guidance System' (2017) *KCNA* http://www.kcna.co.jp/item/2017/201705/news30/20170530-01ee.html
20 Ankit Panda. 'Introducing the KN21, North Korea's New Take on Its Oldest Ballistic Missile' (2017) *The Diplomat* https://thediplomat.com/2017/09/introducing-the-kn21-north-koreas-new-take-on-its-oldest-ballistic-missile/
21 Information obtained from the KPA Exhibition of Arms and Equipment in Pyongyang.
22 Nuclear Threat Initiative. 'North Korean Missile Chronology' (2012) *Nuclear Threat Initiative* https://www.nti.org/media/pdfs/north_korea_missile_2.pdf?_=1327534760?_=1327534760
23 Norbert Brügge. 'The North-Korean/Iranian Nodong-Shahab missile family' *Norbert Brügge* http://www.b14643.de/Spacerockets/Specials/Nodong/index.htm
24 Author interview with Markus Schiller, CEO of ST Analytics GmbH, March 2017.
25 Democratic Voice of Burma. 'Report of Shwe Mann's visit to North Korea' (2010) *DVB* http://www.dvb.no/burmas-nuclear-ambitions/burmas-nuclear-ambitions-military-docs/military-docs/9279
26 Mads Brügger. *The Mole: Undercover in North Korea* (2020) Wingman Media
27 Markus Schiller and Robert H. Schmucker. 'Flashback to the Past: North Korea's "New" Extended-Range Scud' (2016) *38 North* https://www.38north.org/wp-content/uploads/2016/11/Scud-ER-110816_Schiller_Schmucker.pdf
28 Markus Schiller and Robert H. Schmucker. 'Flashback to the Past: North Korea's "New" Extended-Range Scud' (2016) *38 North* https://www.38north.org/wp-content/uploads/2016/11/Scud-ER-110816_Schiller_Schmucker.pdf
29 Information obtained from the KPA Exhibition of Arms and Equipment in Pyongyang.
30 Confusing designations for North Korean R-17 derived missiles abound, and the designators 'Scud-D' and 'Scud-ER' have been associated with this system as well as others. No export name for this missile is known however, and the 'Scud-ER' designation was invented by analysts.
31 Information obtained from the KPA Exhibition of Arms and Equipment in Pyongyang.
32 Nuclear Threat Initiative. 'North Korean Missile Chronology' (2012) *Nuclear Threat Initiative* https://www.nti.org/media/pdfs/north_korea_missile_2.pdf?_=1327534760?_=1327534760
33 Nuclear Threat Initiative. 'North Korean Missile Chronology' (2012) *Nuclear Threat Initiative* https://www.nti.org/media/pdfs/north_korea_missile_2.pdf?_=1327534760?_=1327534760
34 Greg J. Gerardi and James A. Plotts. 'AN ANNOTATED CHRONOLOGY OF DPRK MISSILE TRADE AND DEVELOPMENTS' (1994) *James Martin Center for Nonproliferation Studies* https://www.nonproliferation.org/wp-content/uploads/npr/gerard21.pdf
35 Authors' observation.
36 Hypergolic propellants consist of a fuel component and an oxidiser component which when combined spontaneously ignite to provide thrust. The AK-27I and TM-185 combination used by the Hwasong-5 to Hwasong-9 is actually not hypergolic, and requires a small amount of TG-02 'Tonka' for ignition.
37 Ralph Savelsberg and James Kiessling. 'North Korea's Musudan Missile: A Performance Assessment' (2016) *38 North* http://38north.org/2016/12/musudan122016/
38 Author interview with Markus Schiller, CEO of ST Analytics GmbH, March 2017.
39 Yoon Min Sik. 'NK's IRBM launch fails again' (2016) *The Korea Herald* https://www.koreaherald.com/view.php?ud=20161020000058
40 Jeffrey Lewis. 'Origins of the Musudan IRBM' (2012) *Arms Control Wonk* https://www.armscontrolwonk.com/archive/205337/origins-of-the-musudan-irbm/
41 Democratic Voice of Burma. 'Report of Shwe Mann's visit to North Korea' (2010) *DVB* http://www.dvb.no/burmas-nuclear-ambitions/burmas-nuclear-ambitions-military-docs/military-docs/9279
42 Chad O'Carroll. 'North Korea tried to sell 3,500KM range missiles – arms trader' (2013) *NK News* https://www.nknews.org/2013/06/north-korea-tried-to-sell-3500km-range-missiles-arms-trader/
43 Korea JoongAng Daily. 'North's Missile a Modified SS-21' (2005) *Korea JoongAng Daily* http://koreajoongangdaily.joins.com/news/article/article.aspx?aid=2564031
44 Author interview with Norbert Brügge, missile analyst and author of analysis website www.b14643.de.
45 David Schmerler et al. 'No More Rivet' (2015) *38 North* http://www.38north.org/reports/2015/12/new-icbm-for-nk/section-5/
46 Bill Gertz. 'Iran, North Korea Secretly Developing New Long-Range Rocket Booster for ICBMs' (2013) *The Washington Free Beacon* https://freebeacon.com/national-security/iran-north-korea-secretly-developing-new-long-range-rocket-booster-for-icbms/
47 Korean Central News Agency. 'Kim Jong Un Guides Test-Fire of New Rocket' (2017) *KCNA* http://www.kcna.co.jp/item/2017/201705/news15/20170515-01ee.html
48 In recent years North Korean reports of ballistic missile tests and flight telemetry collected appears to have become more inclusive and accurate, possibly in order to affirm to observers that the claimed capabilities are in fact truthful.
49 Korean Central News Agency. 'Kim Jong Un Inspects KPA Strategic Force Command Element' (2017) *KCNA* http://www.kcna.co.jp/item/2017/201708/news15/20170815-06ee.html

50 Korean Central News Agency. 'Kim Jong Un Guides Second Test-fire of ICBM Hwasong-14' (2017) *KCNA* http://www.kcna.co.jp/item/2017/201707/news29/20170729-04ee.html
51 Michael Elleman. 'North Korea's Hwasong-14 ICBM: New Data Indicates Shorter Range Than Many Thought' (2018) *38 North* https://www.38north.org/2018/11/melleman112918/
52 For missiles of this performance, even tiny design aspects (including the weight of the warhead, heat shield and tank structures) may drastically alter its potential maximum range, making an accurate assessment exceedingly difficult. Analysts have estimated the range to be as low as 6,000 or as high as 8,000 kilometres for a 500 to 600 kilogrammes warhead, with lighter payloads possibly attaining above 10.000 kilometres.
53 Korean Central News Agency. 'Kim Jong Un Guides Ground Jet Test of New-type High-Power Engine of Inter-continental Ballistic Rocket' (2016) *KCNA* http://www.kcna.co.jp/item/2016/201604/news09/20160409-01ee.html
54 Note that prior to 2014, no two-staged missile had ever been tested by the DPRK save for space launch vehicles. Only with the development of the Hwasong-14 in 2017 was a two-staged design of comparable stature finally tested – yet still not a three-staged one.
55 John Schilling. North Korea's Large Rocket Engine Test: A Significant Step Forward for Pyongyang's ICBM Program' (2016) *38 North* https://www.38north.org/2016/04/schilling041116/
56 Since the radius of destruction scales roughly with the cube root of the warhead yield, a single warhead may inflict far less damage than several spaced a distance apart with the same (or smaller) combined yield.
57 Frank Ruediger. 'Key Results of The Eighth Party Congress in North Korea (Part 2 of 2)' (2021) *38 North* https://www.38north.org/2021/01/key-results-of-the-eighth-party-congress-in-north-korea-part-2-of-2/
58 Korean Central News Agency. 'Statement of the General Staff on the conduct of military operations of the KPA in response to the joint air exercises of the United States and South Korea "Vigilant Storm"' (2022) *KCNA* https://dprktoday.com/abroad/news/41400
59 Hyonhee Shin and Josh Smith. 'S.Korea says N.Korea staged 'largest ICBM' fakery to recover from failed test' (2022) *Reuters* https://www.reuters.com/world/asia-pacific/skorea-says-nkorea-staged-largest-icbm-fakery-recover-failed-test-2022-03-30/
60 The same facility appeared to be responsible for the assembly of TELs of a variety of other new ballistic missile systems however, and evidently production of one type virtually ceases whenever that of another commences.
61 Korean Central News Agency. 'Kim Jong Un Guides Ground Test of Jet of High-power Solid-fuel Rocket Engine and Its Cascade Separation' (2016) *KCNA* http://www.kcna.co.jp/item/2016/201603/news24/20160324-02ee.html
62 Korean Central News Agency. 'Kim Jong Un Guides Underwater Test-fire of Strategic Submarine Ballistic Missile' (2016) *KCNA* http://www.kcna.co.jp/item/2016/201604/news24/20160424-01ee.html
63 David Wright. 'Range of the North Korean KN-11 Sub-Launched Missile' (2016) *Union of Concerned Scientists* https://allthingsnuclear.org/dwright/range-of-the-north-korean-kn-11-sub-launched-missile
64 Korean Central News Agency. 'Kim Jong Un Guides Test-fire of Surface-to-surface Medium Long-range Ballistic Missile' (2017) *KCNA* http://www.kcna.co.jp/item/2017/201702/news13/20170213-01ee.html
65 Korean Central News Agency. 'Kim Jong Un Supervises Test-fire of Ballistic Missile' (2017) *KCNA* http://kcna.co.jp/item/2017/201705/news22/20170522-01ee.html
66 Interestingly, the engine nozzle appears to have been made out of a carbon composite, possibly the same 3D carbon/carbon-silicon carbide composite material reported in 2017 to have been developed for the production of ICBM heat shields and solid-fuelled engine nozzles.
Pyongyang Times staff reporter. 'Kim Jong Un inspects defence science institute' (2017) *KCNA Watch* https://kcnawatch.org/newstream/1532002215-554494256/kim-jong-un-inspects-defence-science-institute/
67 British Broadcasting Corporation 'North Korea fires two short-range missiles, South says' (2019) *BBC* https://www.bbc.com/news/world-asia-48212045
68 The introduction of South Korea's Hyunmoo-2B missile, thought to be based on the Iskander itself, is another interesting development to which the new missile system could be reactionary.
69 Tom Balmforth and David Gauthier-Villars. 'Exclusive: Ukraine examines N.Korean missile debris amid fears of Moscow-Pyongyang axis' (2024) *Reuters* https://www.reuters.com/world/ukraine-examines-nkorean-missile-debris-amid-fears-moscow-pyongyang-axis-2024-05-07/
70 Ukraine Field Dispatch. 'North Korean missile relies on recent electronic components' (2024) *Conflict Armament Research* https://storymaps.arcgis.com/stories/0814c6868bbd45a98b15693a31bd0e7f
71 Ukraine Field Dispatch. 'North Korean missiles produced in 2024 used in Ukraine' (2024) *Conflict Armament Research* https://storymaps.arcgis.com/stories/15ae6ca767bc46a1b536ac7e2d962b66
72 Strikes reportedly conducted from the vicinity of Voronezh at the city of Bila Tserkva would suggest a range of at least 660 kilometres.
73 Tom Balmforth. 'Exclusive: Ukraine sees marked improvement in accuracy of Russia's North Korean missiles' (2025) *Reuters* https://www.reuters.com/business/aerospace-defense/ukraine-sees-marked-improvement-accuracy-russias-north-korean-missiles-2025-02-06/
74 Information obtained from reference material held in the authors' archive.
75 KCNA. 'Academy of Defence Science Test-fires New-type Tactical Guided Missiles' (2021) *KCNA Watch* https://kcnawatch.org/newstream/1616726978-436356033/academy-of-defence-science-test-fires-new-type-tactical-guided-missiles/
76 The reports also stated the variant has a minimum range of 90 kilometres.
77 The report erroneously stated 320 kilometres.
78 KCNA. 'DPRK Missile Administration Conducts Test-fire of New-type Tactical Ballistic Missile' (2024) *KCNA Watch* https://kcnawatch.org/newstream/1719871825-376192825/dprk-missile-administration-conducts-test-fire-of-new-type-tactical-ballistic-missile/
79 Rodong Sinmun. 'Commissioning Ceremony of Ultimate Weaponry Demonstrating Sure Victory of Cause of Building Powerful Army Ceremony for Celebrating Transfer and Receiving of New-Type Tactical Ballistic Missile System Takes Place with Splendour' (2024) *KCNA Watch* https://kcnawatch.org/newstream/1722863425-42759958/commissioning-ceremony-of-ultimate-weaponry-demonstrating-sure-victory-of-cause-of-building-powerful-army-ceremony-for-celebrating-transfer-and-receiving-of-new-type-tactical-ballistic-missile-system/
80 The Pyongyang Times. 'DPRK Missile Administration test-fires large-calibre MRLS' (2026) *KCNA Watch* https://kcnawatch.org/newstream/1769764259-605024884/dprk-missile-administration-test-fires-large-calibre-mrls/
81 As can be gleaned from the inscription of 'ㅈㅂㅌ-6' (JBT-6) on its body.
82 Chongnyon Chonwi. 'Respected Comrade Kim Jong Un Gives Field Guidance at Major Munitions Industry Enterprise' (2025) *KCNA Watch* https://kcnawatch.org/newstream/1767078102-713460718/respected-comrade-kim-jong-un-gives-field-guidance-at-major-munitions-industry-enterprise/
83 Decker Eveleth. 'Why guidance systems are the Achilles' heel of North Korea's missile arsenal' (2025) *NK Pro* https://www.nknews.org/pro/why-guidance-systems-are-the-achilles-heel-of-north-koreas-missile-arsenal/
84 Colin Zwirko. 'North Korea launched Hwasong-18 ICBM as show of force against US: State media' (2023) *NK News* https://www.nknews.org/2023/07/north-korea-launched-hwasong-18-icbm-as-show-of-force-against-us-state-media/
85 Assuming a conservative thrust to weight ratio. Its thrust is in fact comparable to that of the US LGM-118 Peacekeeper, which is a smaller design that leverages its high thrust to weight ratio to improve other characteristics.
86 Interestingly, it still featured 12 axles at the time. The most likely explanation is that the (newly introduced) frontmost axle was deemed unnecessary when the vehicle's cabin design was finalised. The fact that these changes were made under two months before its first test are indicative of the breakneck pace and almost haphazard development philosophy that characterises the North Korean ICBM programme.

87 Rodong Sinmun. 'Crucial Test Demonstrating DPRK's Definite Reaction Will and Absolute Superiority of Its Strategic Strike Capability Test-fire of DPRK's Latest-type ICBM Hwasongpho-19 Successfully Conducted under Guidance of Respected Comrade Kim Jong Un' (2024) *KCNA Watch* https://kcnawatch.org/newstream/1730456464-56059927/crucial-test-demonstrating-dprk%e2%80%99s-definite-reaction-will-and-absolute-superiority-of-its-strategic-strike-capability-test-fire-of-dprk%e2-%80%99s-latest-type-icbm-hwasongpho-19-successfully-con/

88 Vann H. Van Diepen. 'North Korea Tests New Solid IRBM With MaRV Payload' (2024) *38 North* https://www.38north.org/2024/01/north-korea-tests-new-solid-irbm-with-marv-payload/

89 Vann H. Van Diepen. 'Second Flight of North Korea's Solid IRBM Also Second Flight of HGV' (2024) *38 North* https://www.38north.org/2024/04/second-flight-of-north-koreas-solid-irbm-also-second-flight-of-hgv/

90 State media coverage in fact showed monitors displaying telemetry suggestive of a range of closer to 1,200 kilometres, casting doubts on the accuracy of either telemetry or the reporting.

91 This time, the telemetry displayed on the monitors seemed to match North Korea's claims.

92 Glocom. 'GR-8422 Data Transceiver' (2024) *Glocom* http://glocom-corp.com/index.php/product/detail?p=gr-8422

93 Chongnyon Chonwi. 'DPRK Missile Administration Succeeds in Test-fire of New-type Intermediate-range Hypersonic Ballistic Missile' (2025) *KCNA Watch* https://kcnawatch.org/newstream/1736236876-529159775/dprk-missile-administration-succeeds-in-test-fire-of-new-type-intermediate-range-hypersonic-ballistic-missile/

94 Joseph S. Bermudez Jr., Victor Cha and Jennifer Jun. 'Changes at North Korean Missile Operating Bases: Part 1' (2024) *Beyond Parallel* https://beyondparallel.csis.org/changes-at-north-korean-missile-operating-bases-part-1/

95 Korean Central News Agency. 'Respected Comrade Kim Jong Un Inspects Strategic Missile Bases' (2024) *KCNA Watch* https://kcnawatch.org/newstream/1729636719-944114134/respected-comrade-kim-jong-un-inspects-strategic-missile-bases/

96 During one test in April 2024 of such a 'super-large' warhead, the system in question was referred to as the Hwasal-1 Ra-3. During another in September 2024, a vertical launch mode was utilised from an obscured TEL, suggesting a new launcher had been developed.

97 Hwasal means Arrow, whereas Pulhwasal means Fire Arrow. The reason for this naming inconsistency is unknown.

98 Hans M. Kristensen and Robert S. Norris. 'A history of US nuclear weapons in South Korea' (2017) *Bulletin of the Atomic Scientists* https://doi.org/10.1080/00963402.2017.1388656

99 Digital Chosun. '"북한, 핵어뢰·핵기뢰 개발중.. 이미 완성 초읽기"' (2010) *Digital Chosun* http://news.chosun.com/site/data/html_dir/2010/12/05/2010120500828.html

100 The recovery of one of the US's Near-Term Mine Reconnaissance System (NMRS) UUVs off the east coast near Hamhung in 2004 might well have prompted North Korea's interest in such devices.

101 Korean Central News Agency. 'Important Weapon Test and Firing Drill Conducted in DPRK' (2023) *KCNA* http://www.uriminzokkiri.com/index.php?lang=eng&ptype=cforev&stype=2&ctype=3&mtype=view&no=46125

102 Korean Central News Agency. 'Underwater Strategic Weapon System Test Held' (2023) *KCNA* http://www.uriminzokkiri.com/index.php?lang=eng&ptype=cfonew&mtype=view&no=46191

103 Colin Zwirko. 'North Korea reveals Haeil-2 undersea 'nuclear attack drone' test for first time' *NK News* https://www.nknews.org/2023/04/north-korea-reveals-haeil-2-undersea-nuclear-attack-drone-test-for-first-time/

104 The second suffix to a North Korean weapons system is believed to specify the warhead type, with for instance Pulhwasal-3-31 believed to refer to a Pulhwasal-3 variant utilising the Hwasan-31 tactical nuclear warhead.

105 This organisation has gone through excessive reorganisations as well, being known as the Korean Committee of Space Technology before 2013, and the National Aerospace Development Administration in the period intervening up to 2023. Please excuse the writers if another idiosyncratic name change occurs between the time of publishing and reading.

106 Choe Sang-Hun. 'Kim Jong-un Wants a Satellite in Space. Seoul Says He Has a Long Way to Go', (2023) *The New York Times* https://www.nytimes.com/2023/07/05/world/asia/north-korea-spy-satellite-useless-failure.html

107 Marco Langbroek. ' A perigee-raising manoeuvre by the North Korean satellite Malligyong-1' (2024) *SatTrackCam Leiden (b) log* https://sattrackcam.blogspot.com/2024/02/a-perigee-raising-manoeuvre-by-north.html

108 It should be noted of these failures that North Korea utilises an excessively complicated launch profile in order to avoid overflying its neighbours, with each stage making significant course corrections.

109 Glocom. 'GS-2600-06xx Datalink/Telemetry System' (2024) *Glocom* http://glocom-corp.com/index.php/product/detail?p=gs-2600-06

110 Andrei Gromyko. 'FROM THE JOURNAL OF GROMYKO, RECORD OF A CONVERSATION WITH AMBASSADOR RI SIN-PAL OF THE DEMOCRATIC PEOPLE'S REPUBLIC OF KOREA' (1958) *Wilson Center* https://digitalarchive.wilsoncenter.org/document/116019

111 Nuclear Threat Initiative. 'North Korea Nuclear Chronology' (2011) *Nuclear Threat Initiative* https://media.nti.org/pdfs/north_korea_nuclear.pdf

112 János Taraba. 'REPORT, EMBASSY OF HUNGARY IN NORTH KOREA TO THE HUNGARIAN FOREIGN MINISTRY' (1985) *Wilson Center* https://digitalarchive.wilsoncenter.org/document/110142

113 Nuclear Threat Initiative. 'North Korea Nuclear Chronology' (2011) *Nuclear Threat Initiative* https://media.nti.org/pdfs/north_korea_nuclear.pdf

114 François Carrel-Billiard and Christine Wing, 'Nuclear Energy, Nonproliferation, and Disarmament: Briefing Notes for the 2010 NPT Review Conference', (2010) *International Peace Institute* https://www.ipinst.org/wp-content/uploads/2010/04/pdfs_koreachapt2.pdf

115 Nuclear Threat Initiative. 'North Korea Nuclear Chronology' (2011) *Nuclear Threat Initiative* https://media.nti.org/pdfs/north_korea_nuclear.pdf

116 Joseph S. Bermudez Jr., Victor Cha and Jennifer Jun. 'Punggye-ri Declassified: Birth of North Korea's "Northern Nuclear Testing Site"' https://beyondparallel.csis.org/punggye-ri-declassified-birth-of-north-koreas-northern-nuclear-testing-site/

117 Korean Central News Agency. 'Statement of DPRK Government on its withdrawal from NPT' (2003) *KCNA* www.kcna.co.jp/item/2003/200301/news01/11.htm

118 Nuclear Threat Initiative. 'North Korea Nuclear Chronology' (2011) *Nuclear Threat Initiative* https://media.nti.org/pdfs/north_korea_nuclear.pdf

119 Jamie McIntyre. 'Washington was on brink of war with North Korea 5 years ago' (1999) *CNN* http://edition.cnn.com/US/9910/04/korea.brink/

120 De Geer, LE., Wright, C.M. & Robertson, L. Establishing the case for a May 2010 low-yield, unannounced nuclear test in North Korea. *J Radioanal Nucl Chem* 334, 1067–1084 (2025). https://doi.org/10.1007/s10967-024-09453-2

121 Korean Central News Agency. 'KCNA Report on Successful 3rd Underground Nuclear Test' (2013) *KCNA* http://www.kcna.co.jp/item/2013/201302/news12/20130212-18ee.html

122 Korean Central News Agency. 'DPRK Proves Successful in H-bomb Test' (2016) *KCNA* http://www.kcna.co.jp/item/2016/201601/news06/20160106-12ee.html

123 Estimated to have been smaller than 10 kilotonnes of TNT, whereas a hydrogen bomb (usually taken to be synonymous with a thermonuclear weapon) typically releases energies in the megatonnes range – a yield over a hundred times larger.

124 Korean Central News Agency. 'DPRK Nuclear Weapons Institute on Successful Test of H-bomb for ICBM' (2017) *KCNA* http://www.kcna.co.jp/item/2017/201709/news03/20170903-13ee.html

125 Karl Dewey, et al. 'North Korea bargains with nuclear diplomacy' (2017) *IHS Jane's* http://www.janes.com/images/assets/111/75111/North_Korea_bargains_with_nuclear_diplomacy.pdf

126 Korean Central News Agency. 'DPRK Nuclear Weapons Institute on Successful Test of H-bomb for ICBM' (2017) *KCNA* http://www.kcna.co.jp/item/2017/201709/news03/20170903-13ee.html

127 Kim Yo Jong. 'Is It "Boast of Strength" by Group of Curs or Funeral Procession of Colonial Mercenary Army' (2024) *Korean Central News Agency* http://kcna.kp/en/article/q/33635294de828ec4db1543b250cd6946.kcmsf
128 Hans M. Kristensen, Matt Korda, Eliana Johns and Mackenzie Knight. 'North Korean nuclear weapons, 2024' (2024) *Bulletin of the Atomic Scientists* https://doi.org/10.1080/00963402.2024.2365013
129 Rodong Sinmun. 'Respected Comrade Kim Jong Un Inspects Nuclear Weapons Institute and Production Base of Weapons-grade Nuclear Materials' (2024) *KCNA Watch* https://kcnawatch.org/newstream/1726224616-578642831/respected-comrade-kim-jong-un-inspects-nuclear-weapons-institute-and-production-base-of-weapons-grade-nuclear-materials/
130 Siegfried S. Hecker and Robert L. Carlin. 'Siegfried S. Hecker and Robert L. Carlin' (2024) *38North* https://www.38north.org/2024/09/a-closer-look-at-north-koreas-enrichment-capabilities-and-what-it-means/
131 Jeffrey Lewis and Sam Lair. 'A New Enrichment Plant At Yongbyon?' (2025) *Arms Control Wonk* https://www.armscontrolwonk.com/archive/1220487/a-new-enrichment-plant-at-yongbyon/
132 Korean Central News Agency. 'WPK Central Committee Issues Order to Conduct First H-Bomb Test' (2016) *KCNA* www.kcna.co.jp/item/2016/201601/news06/20160106-11ee.html
133 Korean Central News Agency. ' Law on Consolidating Position of Nuclear Weapons State Adopted' (2013) *KCNA* http://kcna.co.jp/item/2013/201304/news01/20130401-25ee.html
134 Korean Central News Agency. 'Law on DPRK's Policy on Nuclear Forces Promulgated' (2022) *KCNA* http://kcna.co.jp/item/2022/202209/news09/20220909-02ee.html
135 To use a popular comparison, roughly 10 times the explosive power of the atomic bomb dropped on Hiroshima during the Second World War.
136 Colin Zwirko. 'North Korea says it successfully tested multiple warhead missile system' (2024) *NK News* https://www.nknews.org/2024/06/north-korea-says-it-successfully-conducted-multiple-warhead-missile-test/
137 The USA reserves the right to retaliate against any state that does not observe the Geneva Protocol, but such use is still banned under the CWC of which it is a signatory.
138 Joseph S. Bermudez Jr., *Shield of the Great Leader: The Armed Forces of North Korea* (St Leonards NSW: Allen & Unwin, 2001)
139 Hyun-Kyung Kim, et al. 'North Korea's Biological Weapons Program' (2017) *Belfer Center for Science and International Affairs* https://www.belfercenter.org/sites/default/files/2017-10/NK%20Bioweapons%20final.pdf
140 Obviously, the DPRK does not distribute evidence of such comments through its media. The veracity of these statements, which at various times have alleged that Kim Il Sung found nuclear, chemical, biological and tunnel warfare to be the most effective, is therefore often doubtful.
141 Nuclear Threat Initiative. 'North Korea Biological Chronology' (2012) *Nuclear Threat Initiative* http://www.nti.org/media/pdfs/north_korea_biological_1.pdf?_=1344293752
142 This 14th pathogen does not appear in most literature, except for the 2012 ROK MoD white paper.
143 Hyun-Kyung Kim, et al. 'North Korea's Biological Weapons Program' (2017) *Belfer Center for Science and International Affairs*
144 Republic of Korea Ministry of National Defense. 'Defense White Paper 2016' *ROK MoD* http://www.mnd.go.kr/mbshome/mbs/mndEN/
145 Hyun-Kyung Kim, et al. 'North Korea's Biological Weapons Program' (2017) *Belfer Center for Science and International Affairs*
146 Melissa Hanham. 'Kim Jong Un Tours Pesticide Facility Capable of Producing Biological Weapons: A 38 North Special Report' (2015) *38 North* https://www.38north.org/2015/07/mhanham070915/
147 Republic of Korea Ministry of National Defense. 'Defense White Paper 2016' *ROK MoD* http://www.mnd.go.kr/mbshome/mbs/mndEN/
148 Jung Min-ho. 'Anthrax vaccine under review for approval amid terrorism concerns' (2025) *The Korea Times* https://www.koreatimes.co.kr/www/nation/2025/01/113_385132.html
149 US Department of Defense. 'Clarifying Guidance for Smallpox and Anthrax Vaccine Immunization Programs' (2015) *US Department of Defense* https://www.health.mil/Reference-Center/Policies/2015/11/12/Clarifying-Guidance-for-Smallpox-and-Anthrax-Vaccine-Immunization-Programs
150 Nuclear Threat Initiative. 'North Korea Chemical Chronology' (2012) *Nuclear Threat Initiative* http://www.nti.org/media/pdfs/north_korea_chemical_chron.pdf?_=1349468965
151 Nuclear Threat Initiative. 'North Korea Chemical Chronology' (2012) *Nuclear Threat Initiative* http://www.nti.org/media/pdfs/north_korea_chemical_chron.pdf?_=1349468965
152 Reportedly from the Soviet Union and German Democratic Republic, respectively.
153 Nuclear Threat Initiative. 'North Korea Chemical Chronology' (2012) *Nuclear Threat Initiative* http://www.nti.org/media/pdfs/north_korea_chemical_chron.pdf?_=1349468965
154 Nowadays, this would amount to the largest stockpiles in possession by any nation in the world.
155 Authors' observation.
156 Nuclear Threat Initiative. 'North Korea Chemical Chronology' (2012) *Nuclear Threat Initiative* http://www.nti.org/media/pdfs/north_korea_chemical_chron.pdf?_=1349468965
157 United Nations Security Council. 'Report of the Panel of Experts established pursuant to resolution 1874 (2009)' 27 February 2017 *UNSC*
158 Marcel Serr. 'North Korea Built a Nuclear Reactor for Syria (And Israel Destroyed It)' (2018) *The National Interest* https://nationalinterest.org/blog/the-buzz/north-korea-built-nuclear-reactor-syria-israel-destroyed-it-23922
159 Nuclear Threat Initiative. 'Al-Kibar Facility' (2011) *Nuclear Threat Initiative* https://www.nti.org/learn/facilities/461/
160 United Nations Security Council. 'Report of the Panel of Experts established pursuant to resolution 1874 (2009)' 5 March 2018 *UNSC*

ABOUT THE AUTHORS

Joost Oliemans is an analyst and author focussing on Asia, the Middle East and North Africa. Together with Stijn Mitzer, he is the author of *The Armed Forces of North Korea: On The Path of Songun*. Joost Oliemans also writes for various news agencies and websites about military-related matters.

Stijn Mitzer is a conflict analyst specialising in modern-day weaponry and military tactics, especially in relation to active warzones and military hot spots. His extensive experience in covering today's conflicts has resulted in an in-depth knowledge of currently relevant trends in warfare, as well as a clear perception of the military situation in virtually any country. Having worked for open-source intelligence websites such as Janes, Bellingcat and NK News, he runs the independent analysis website www.oryxspioenkop.com with his co-author Joost Oliemans, and authored *The Armed Forces of North Korea: On The Path of Songun*.